GREAT PEOPLE IN HISTORY

GREAT PHILOSOPHERS

GREAT PEOPLE IN HISTORY

GREAT PHILOSOPHERS

JEREMY STANGROOM
JAMES GARVEY

ROSEN
PUBLISHING®
New York

This edition published in 2013 by:

The Rosen Publishing Group, Inc.
29 East 21st Street, New York, NY 10010

Copyright © 2013 Arcturus Publishing Limited

Library of Congress Cataloging-in-Publication Data

Stangroom, Jeremy.
Great philosophers / Jeremy Stangroom, James Garvey.
p. cm. -- (Great people in history)
Includes bibliographical references and index.
ISBN 978-1-4777-0404-2 (library binding)
1. Philosophy--History. 2. Philosophers. I. Garvey, James, 1967- II. Title.
B72.S7825 2013
190--dc23
2012032781

Manufactured in China

SL002555US

Compliance Information: Batch W13YA:
For further information, contact Rosen Publishing, New York,
New York, at 1-800-237-9932

Contents

Introduction

No one is entirely sure what philosophy is. If that's not a reassuring first sentence in a book on many of the world's greatest philosophers, it's at least an honest one. There are three sorts of view of what philosophy is, and no broad agreement about which one is right. It's worth wondering about these three answers a little.

Some maintain that philosophy is best defined by its abstract subject matter. Philosophy as traditionally conceived deals with the Big Three Questions. What exists? How do we know? What are we going to do about it? The answers involve us in metaphysics, the study of the nature of reality; epistemology, the study of the conditions required to know something; and ethics, an attempt to say what it is to live a morally good life. These are distinctly human questions in the sense that it is hard to be human without wondering about them at some time or other. Great minds sometimes settle on them, think about them, and the result is philosophy.

Some argue instead that one might philosophize about anything, that philosophy is best defined by a particular method. The method has a lot to do with careful and systematic thinking, giving reasons for conclusions, and getting those conclusions into clear view. Anyone can have a view about what's right or wrong, but the view becomes philosophy if it is explicitly characterized, has some support in reason.

Finally, some take it that philosophy consists in a kind of attitude or way of life. Distinctive of this way of living is a critical view of things, a refusal to accept what others accept without further reflection. It has got more than one great philosopher into serious trouble. One example here is Socrates, who thought that the unexamined life was not worth living. He not only thought this, he died for it. Many join him in thinking that the word 'philosophy', literally 'love of wisdom', marks out an approach to life as against a method or set of questions.

Someone who plumps for any of these answers will be happy to find representatives of his or her view in this book. Certainly answers to all three Big Questions get a lot of attention, as does the distinctive method of philosophy, as do the lives of philosophers. There is tension here, too, and it's impossible to resolve it. Fans of method will be annoyed to find Nietzsche and Hegel on the list. Proponents of the subject-matter view might blanch at the inclusion of Machiavelli. Those who see philosophy as a way of life will wonder about Bacon and Heidegger.

Nevertheless, the list hangs together. If it's hard to say just what philosophy is, it's easy to spot when you see it. Wittgenstein argues that some terms pick things out not in virtue of a strict definition, but by something like family resemblance. Maybe not everyone in the family album sports a version of grandfather's admirable nose, but it's clear that all are members of the same family. So too with the great philosophers. Philosophy has been under way for more than two thousand years, and in such a long stretch, it would be something of a miracle if all philosophers fitted a single mold.

This book traces the biggest thoughts in the largest and most influential parts of philosophy's long walk through history. You will find here thinkers of the first philosophical thoughts in the West, the Ancient Greek and Early Roman philosophers to whom so much is owed. You will see the way in which their concerns became the concerns of those who followed; the way their answers shaped what we now recognize as philosophy. Medieval philosophy makes an appearance, carrying ancient concerns on to Renaissance philosophers, adding an emphasis on religion to the mix. The thinking of the modern era, the modern explosion of philosophy ushered in by Descartes, is well represented here too. Founders and representatives of the rationalist and empiricist schools get a fair hearing, as do the dark conclusions of those who favour skepticism.

The long walk is, thankfully, carrying on, and you will find here the thoughts which make contemporary philosophy what it is, and perhaps what it is on the way to becoming. Philosophy, whatever it is, is certainly still under way, and this book takes account of both the discipline as it is practiced now and the history which made contemporary philosophy possible.

Usually, the introduction to a book like this offers some sort of apology for cutting corners, says that it's impossible to characterize fully the thoughts of so many great philosophers in a single place. You also find apologies of another sort, excuses for including some philosophers and not others. You will find no apologies for such obvious and unavoidable facts here. Does it make any sense at all to apologize for a fact or set of facts? This book is written for intelligent people who know what they're getting into when they read a book. If this book is not the last word on the great philosophers – and what book possibly could be – it is certainly a collection of useful first words. Included with each entry is a list of works you can read if you want to take your study of philosophy further. You won't find any last words there either.

No matter how you view philosophy, regardless of what you think it is, you have here accounts of the lives and thoughts of the very best thinkers in the philosophical neighborhood, dealing carefully and rationally with the most human of questions, the hardest questions, the questions which matter most.

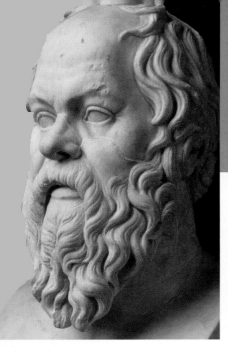

Socrates

It would be difficult to overestimate the influence of Socrates (470–399 BCE) on Western philosophy. We know that Socrates was the mentor of the young Plato, and we also know that Plato's writings had deep and lasting effects on virtually the whole of Western thinking.

470–399 BCE

Irritatingly, it would also be difficult to overestimate our ignorance of Socrates' actual views. Socrates probably wrote next to nothing of a philosophical nature, and, anyway, none of it survives. Our problem, the "Socratic Problem" as it is called, is that we do not know exactly what Socrates himself believed—it is not clear that he claims to know anything. He even denies being a teacher. So we know he is massively influential, but we do not know the precise nature of that influence. The situation is more than exasperating.

Socrates is believed to have been the son of a midwife and a stonemason. Although he was reduced to poverty in old age, he seems to have enjoyed a reasonably well-off early life. He served as a hoplite (a heavy infantryman) in the Athenian army, so at least at that time in his life he must have owned property and been able to pay for his own equipment. However he made his living, it was not by his looks. He is described variously as pug-nosed, rotund, and with bulbous eyes, and he seems not to have been devoted to personal grooming.

If what interests us is not his life but his views, there are only three contenders, three reasonable sources of information about Socrates' philosophy, three writers alive in his lifetime. The comic poet Aristophanes is one, but he paints a ridiculous portrait of Socrates, a general caricature and amalgam of philosophers and intellectuals active in Athens at the time. The writings of Xenophon survive, but he characterizes Socrates as nothing more than a vapid repository of homey aphorisms—one wonders how such a man could have troubled the Athenian authorities as much as Socrates in fact did. We have, finally, the dialogues of Plato, but even these are problematic. We will follow convention and assume with most commentators (and with a large pinch of salt) that the Socrates of Plato's early dialogues is as near a faithful representation of the views of the actual Socrates as we are likely to have.

However Socrates made his living, it was not by his looks; he is described variously as pug-nosed, thick-lipped, and rotund

A New Approach

From those early dialogues, something of the man's views emerges. It is clear that we call those who came before Socrates "Pre-Socratic" for a reason: his interests differ markedly from the preoccupations of the earlier philosophers such as Parmenides, Heraclitus, and Anaximander. Rather than speculate on cosmology, affecting dark pronouncements on the nature of the Absolute, Socrates was "the first to call philosophy down from the heavens," in Cicero's memorable phrase. Socrates worries about this life and how best to live it. His concerns are resolutely practical.

The Early Dialogues

The Socrates of the early dialogues typically strikes up a conversation with one or a few interlocutors, which eventuates in a question about the nature of some virtue or other: what is justice, what is piety, what is courage, or what is temperance. The interlocutor attempts an answer. Socrates then subjects the answer to critical analysis, usually showing that the answer is inconsistent with something else held by the interlocutor to be true, that it leads to some confusion or other or is plainly lacking in some respect. The Greek word for this pattern of questioning, responding, and scrutinizing is "*elenchus*," and Socrates was a master of it. According to Xenophon, he "could do what he liked with any disputant." Why did he engage in the elenchus? There are a number of answers.

According to one legend, Chaerephon asks the Oracle at Delphi whether anyone is wiser than Socrates, and the surprising answer is that no one is wiser. Socrates, astonished, tries to prove the Oracle wrong by approaching those who profess wisdom and asking them about the virtues. When he reduces each one to confusion, he concludes that the Oracle is right, in a way: Socrates knows he doesn't know anything, whereas others are wrong in thinking they know.

The point of the many encounters, the many arguments, cannot just consist in undermining the self-confidence of prominent Athenians, and indeed we have some hints from the dialogues of Socrates' view of his own activity. Perhaps Socrates really is pursuing definitions. It certainly seems, in places, as though he thinks that only with such definitions in hand can one have the knowledge required to make the right choices in life. Unless we know what justice is, how can we possibly hope to act justly?

We do have the problem of reconciling the fact that Socrates never clearly settles upon a definition, yet he does not consider his efforts failures. The dialogues do not end with a crestfallen Socrates, head in hands, bemoaning his ineptitude. On the contrary, there is often a kind of upbeat satisfaction, even gratitude shown all around to those who

MAJOR WORKS

Socrates wrote nothing of a philosophical nature. We can, however, look to Plato's early dialogues—which some take to express Socrates' actual views—for guidance. The following three dialogues together give an account of part of Socrates' philosophy and the way he faced his death. We cannot say just when any were written.

Apology contains Socrates' defense in response to charges of corrupting the youth of Athens and impiety.

He also talks about his beliefs and convictions and the life he has led.

Crito recounts a conversation between Socrates and his friend Crito, which conveys something of Socrates' ethical views.

Phaedo is a very moving account of Socrates' final hours and contains discussions of immortality, the soul, and death.

have taken the time to reflect with him, something approaching joy and the recognition of time very well spent. Engaging in the cooperative pursuit of definitions is not only of value to him, it is of extraordinary value: the unexamined life, Socrates says as he nears his death, is not worth living. Yet if the aim of the exercise is getting definitions, the examined life is a kind of failure. There is at least one way to resolve this depressing conclusion.

It might well be that a stable definition is not the point and purpose of the exercise at all; perhaps the activity of joint inquiry itself is the aim, examination itself is of value. In other words, it may be that Socrates finds value not in getting at the truth, but looking for it in conversation. One might reasonably wonder why he thinks this. Some maintain that instilling in his companions not truth, but the desire for truth, was the point in the first place. It is worth noting that philosophy as it is conducted now still has a share in this. Lectures at university are accompanied by seminars aimed at discussion. Talks at conferences are followed by questions and answers. Philosophy is still the collective enterprise it was in Socrates' day. Perhaps this is a kind of vindication of this view of his activities.

Socratic Paradoxes

Although no clear and stable definitions materialize, there are some themes, if certainly not doctrines, that emerge in the early dialogues which we might reasonably take to be Socratic. There are many formulations of the so-called "Socratic paradox" or "Socratic paradoxes": no one does wrong voluntarily or deliberately; virtue is knowledge; moral weakness is impossible. The line of thought underpinning all versions is this. What is good is beneficial and what is evil or wrong is harmful to us. Doing wrong hurts us, damages what is most valuable in us—our soul. No one really desires what is harmful unless he fails to recognize it as such, unless he mistakes it for something beneficial. All wrongdoing, then, results from ignorance. No one who really knows virtue will act immorally; no one who really understands right and wrong will chose anything other than what is right. Anyone who, in fact, chooses to do something morally wrong does so only in ignorance.

Would this view have been a comfort to Socrates who, at the age of seventy, faced his accusers on charges of impiety and corrupting the youth of Athens? It is hard not to wonder. We can do more than wonder about the charges. Socrates professed to have a kind of mystical, divine sign—perhaps something like an inner voice—which warned him against some actions. The Delphic Oracle's pronouncements might have been taken by him as a kind of holy mission. Both of these possibilities might explain a part of the impiety claim.

In what sense did he corrupt the youth? As you might imagine, speculation has abounded. He certainly did gather around him a circle of young men, many the sons of prominent Athenians, quite of few of them staunch antidemocrats. When democratic feeling ran high, it is possible that excuses for the boys' unpopular views were found in the influence of Socrates.

We can also do more than wonder about the motivations of his accusers. Certainly his practice of asking prominent Athenians awkward questions, in broad daylight and in public, about the nature of virtue, reducing them to confusion, suffusing his interrogations with well-known Socratic irony, could not have won him many influential friends. It is likely that the intention of his accusers consisted in little more than shutting him up. In Plato's record of the trial, it is clear that if only Socrates would agree to stop his philosophizing, he would be free to go, but this is, of course, the one thing he simply could not do. When given the chance to plead for his life, recommend a punishment for himself other than death, Socrates offers his judges an ethics primer. He suggests that his good works—his interrogations, which have done nothing but improve the moral health of the citizens and therefore the city of Athens—can only be rewarded by putting him up at the expense of the city itself in these, his declining years. He seems to have left his judges with no alternative but to condemn him to death. He refuses the opportunity to flee. He drinks the poison and dies.

The Death of Socrates. Socrates comforts his grieving friends by reaffirming his belief in a true and unchanging reality beyond the earthly realm.

If we cannot say, exactly, what doctrines Socrates held or how he lived, we know at least from the dialogues that Plato loved him, whoever he was. The portrait he paints is profoundly affectionate. Socrates might have been physically unappealing, but it is hard to imagine a more attractive character: the good humor and conviviality; the devastating skill in debate; the passion for knowledge or at least the will to pursue it anywhere and anytime; patience with those keen to know and little time for fools; the oddness; the integrity that cost him his life.

It is easy to be drawn into the debate, to smile and quietly cheer for Socrates as he brings low some over-stuffed, jet-setting Athenian; to read again difficult parts of his replies in the hope of better understanding him; to put the book down and stare out a bus window, wondering what Socrates would have said had so-and-so replied to his question a little differently. You can easily understand what good company he must have been. Had you been there—sitting in the Athenian sun, listening to the arguments—you would have been corrupted too. No doubt this has much to do with Plato's art, but it is impossible not to suppose, too, that it has something to do with the personality of Socrates.

It is easy to be drawn into the debate, to cheer for Socrates as he brings low some over-stuffed, jet-setting Athenian

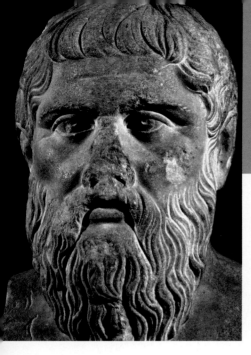

Plato

It is possible to argue about who is the finest Renaissance painter. It is possible to argue in this way about sculptors, writers, poets, more or less any sort of artist. However, if the question is who writes the best dialogues, then there is no room for controversy. Plato (428–347 BCE) has no peers.

428–347 BCE

While it is true that a handful of philosophers have had a stab at writing dialogues, and some such works are of serious philosophical interest, there really is no comparing them to Plato's writings. Plato has the possibly singular distinction of simultaneously inventing and bringing to perfection a kind of art.

It is clear that things might have been different. Plato was probably destined for a career in politics or at least public life. His father, Ariston, was allegedly descended from the last king of Athens. Some sources report that his mother, Perictione, was a relative of the Athenian statesman Solon. When his father died, Plato's mother married a friend of Pericles. Plato had an impressive pedigree, and his family was well connected and wealthy. It is sometimes said that the injustice surrounding the execution of Plato's mentor, Socrates, led Plato to reject public life and pursue philosophy. We know that Plato and some of his relatives and associates were staunch antidemocrats, and following the fall of the Thirty Tyrants, antidemocratic sentiments were not rewarded in Athens. So it is also possible that it was the lack of opportunity for people with his political leanings that kept Plato out of political life. We simply do not know.

Early Life

Little is known about much of Plato's life. It is likely that he undertook military service, possibly as a member of the Athenian cavalry in action against Sparta. The image of Plato thundering into battle on horseback is not an easy one to come to grips with, but it is worth remembering that "Plato" was a nickname, meaning "broad" or "wide"—a reference to his broad shoulders. So he might have been something of a warrior. His actual name was Aristolces. But for a nickname that stuck, English might have been lumbered with "Aristolcic relationships."

We know that he traveled, probably to Egypt and certainly to Syracuse. Seneca reports that he suffered an illness as a result of his travels late in life, but whether or not this killed him is an open question—it seems unlikely. We also know that he and a few others founded the Academy in 385 BCE, widely considered the first university but probably nothing of the sort. According to some reports, "The Academy" was actually the name of Plato's house, and it seems likely that he and only a few like-minded individuals took on a small number of students and offered private tuition. It is not clear that Plato actually lectured there—in his writings, Aristotle, a student at the Academy for twenty years, mentions only the dialogues when considering Plato's views, as opposed to lectures or discussion. At any rate, the place would have been unlike a modern or even medieval university in nearly all respects. Nevertheless, it did have a remarkable lifespan, continuing for nine hundred years. That tireless promoter of Christianity, the Roman Emperor Justinian, considered it a pagan institution and saw to it that its doors were finally and permanently closed.

If little reliable information about his life has come down to us, we are staggeringly fortunate in having probably all the dialogues he wrote. They are usually organized into at least three periods, though the precise ordering is a matter of continuing controversy. Socrates is the main figure and hero in most. The so-called "early" dialogues are thought to reflect the historical Socrates' own interests, but in the middle and later periods Socrates becomes more and more a mouthpiece for Plato. Nevertheless, it is clear that Socrates casts a very long shadow over Plato, and some of Plato's most profound insights are attempts to deal with Socratic worries, or at least worries emerging from Socratic interests.

Although we use the word "blue," how did we learn to do so, when we never encounter an unambiguous example?

Defining the Virtues

The early dialogues have Socrates searching for definitions of the virtues, motivated by the view that one must know what, for example, justice is before one can hope to act justly. It is worth noting that Socrates never finds an acceptable definition, and it is possible that this raises a difficulty which Plato's middle and later works attempt to answer. Other difficulties, closely connected, probably motivated Plato too. We will have a look at a few of them; for example, our use of a general term like "blue."

We apply the word "blue" to a variety of things, but how on earth did we learn to do so when we never actually encounter an unambiguous example of blue? Everything we see is blue and cold or blue and bitter or blue and small: how then did we learn to use the word "blue" in the first place?

MAJOR WORKS

We probably have all of Plato's dialogues, but we really cannot say when each one was written. The following are among the most important of Plato's works.

Republic is without doubt Plato's masterpiece. It begins with a consideration of the nature of justice and quickly becomes an extended consideration of politics, epistemology, and much else.

Symposium is not representative of the dialogues, containing as it does a series of speeches at a dinner party, rather than the full-on Socratic debate of most of Plato's other dialogues, but it is among the most beautiful things ever written. It takes as its topic the nature of love.

Meno deals with virtue, knowledge, and the relation between them.

Parmenides contains an interesting critique of Plato's Theory of Forms, including the famous Third Man Argument. It is worth reading if only for the opportunity to see Socrates seem to lose an argument.

Theaetetus takes up the topics of knowledge and wisdom. It concludes with some instructive thoughts on the point of Socratic dialectic.

Or consider what we take to be our knowledge of something blue, let us say, for instance, my mundane knowledge that my shirt is blue. It is fairly clear that the world around us is constantly changing. My blue shirt will be washed and washed; it will begin to fade, and soon it won't really be the same fetching blue that it is today. I might inadvertently wash it with something else that is not color-fast, something bright orange, in which case my faded shirt will not even be blue at all. Regrettably, in the fullness of time, it won't even be a shirt anymore, returning, as all things must, to dust. Two questions arise from all this.

First, as my shirt fades, what standard do we use to say, truly, that it is not as blue as it was? As my shirt falls apart and looks less and less like a shirt (perhaps more and more like a rag), what standard do we use to say, truly, that it is not a shirt anymore? Some unchanging standard seems needed to make sense of these judgments, but what could do the job in this changing world?

If something is truly known, it is known forever; it cannot turn out to be false tomorrow

Second, it seems that a proposition known could never become false. Opinions certainly could change, as do fashions, but if knowledge is possible, the objects of knowledge must themselves be unchanging. If something is known, it is known forever. "Two plus two equals four," "Triangles have three sides," "Bachelors are unmarried, adult males": all these propositions are true, and they cannot turn out to be false tomorrow. Knowledge, thought Plato, is above the fluctuating vagaries of this imperfect world. How could this be? What ensures that knowledge is fixed, if everything around us is constantly changing?

The Theory of Forms

Plato's Theory of Forms is an attempt to deal with all of this, and the solution is radical. He claims that real, mind-independent entities exist—forms of things like Justice, Good, Beauty, Triangle, Blue, Bachelor, and so on for any general term you like. Socratic interviews really do aim at truth; there are definitions; there is knowledge; words can be learned; standards underpin judgment; all because there are timeless, stable, perfect, unchanging, intelligible things: Forms. We can hope for an understanding of justice because, literally, Justice exists.

Although you will not find Justice in this vale of tears, you can find acts, people, events, and laws that, in some sense, resemble or share in or participate in the Form Justice—indeed, it is this that makes all such things just. You will never see perfect Justice, only shadowy copies, but you might come to an intellectual grasp of Justice by engaging in Socratic dialectic, which now has objects at which to aim. You cannot really be said to know anything about this imperfect world, but the unchanging Forms make possible genuine knowledge of the Good, the Beautiful, and so on. Perfect standards for judgments exist too: one who grasps the Beautiful, say, will be so much the better judge of the shadowy reflections of Beauty in this world.

The Theory of the Forms gets an awful lot of press, but it is true that it only appears in the middle dialogues, and Plato criticizes the view himself in the later dialogues. The best known objection to the theory, the Third Man Argument, runs as follows. Beautiful things in this world are beautiful just in so far as they participate in or resemble the Form of the Beautiful. The Form of the Beautiful, Plato alleges, is itself beautiful. Does this not require some third Form which the Beautiful itself resembles? Socrates and Milo are both men because they resemble something else, the Form Man. But the Form Man must also be a man (or share in manhood), just as the Beautiful itself is beautiful. Does this not require a third thing, a Third Man, which the Form Man must resemble in order for it, too, to be a man? The regress thus initiated looks viscous and infinite.

The Theory of Forms, whether or not it overcomes this objection, figures in many of Plato's dialogues. Although it might be an oversimplification, some argue that the theory provides him with the groundwork for almost everything else he writes about, and the breadth of Plato's philosophical interests is genuinely astonishing. He formulates a general metaphysical outlook, a conception of the soul as immortal (and thus able to visit the realm of Forms), a view of learning as recollection, a complex epistemology, a theory of mathematics, an objectivist ethics, a highly detailed and nuanced (if perhaps disturbing) political philosophy, views on society, a theory of mind, a methodology. Think of any of the usual subdivisions of philosophical inquiry, and Plato has a view on at least a part of it.

Plato's Importance

A.N. Whitehead famously remarked that the safest characterization of Western thought is that "it consists of a series of footnotes to Plato." It has been said since that this is an exaggeration, but not an outrageous one. Others find Plato a little wishy-washy, preferring the tough-minded and careful analysis of Aristotle to the allegorical excesses of Plato's dialogues. Some grumble a little and say they would rather have the beauty of an argument than the beauty of a metaphor. Whatever one makes of the value of Plato's writings, it is clear that they have traveled well. One still smiles and grimaces, agrees and objects, at all the right places, all the places Plato intended when he wrote the dialogues two thousand years ago. It is difficult to imagine anyone writing today who will be read in 4,000 CE. If there is anything like a university around in that distant year, it is sometimes said, we can be certain that Plato will be required reading.

THE CAVE

The fire

The Roadway

Diffused daylight →

Ascent to sunlight

The Myth of the Cave is the metaphor that Plato used to describe his Theory of Forms. Plato's prisoners sit and watch the shadowplay on the wall of the cave, convinced that what they are seeing is reality.

Aristotle

Imagine that you are Plato, coming to the end of your years, presiding over the now-famous Academy, enjoying a reputation among both your students in particular and Athenians in general. You hear, perhaps while lingering in a doorway, a murmured reference to the "Reader," the "Mind of the Academy."

384–322 BCE

They are not talking about you, but a young upstart from the sticks, perhaps only seventeen years old, called "Aristotle." Would you find this galling?

In truth, we can only speculate about the relationship between Plato and Aristotle (384–322 BCE). We know that Aristotle's father, a physician to the court of the King of Macedon, sent him to Athens when he was about seventeen and that he joined the Academy, remaining there for twenty years, first as a student and eventually as a teacher. In the year that Plato died, Aristotle departed—no one knows whether he remained out of loyalty to Plato and left on the master's death, or departed in disgust, having not been offered control of the school. We do know that his father's connections led him to Macedonia, to tutor a thirteen-year-old, the future Alexander the Great.

After years of travel and study, he returned to Athens and founded the Lyceum or peripatetic school—so named either because lectures were conducted on the move or in honor of the locale's fine walkways. Here he remained until 323 BCE, when, so the story goes, his Macedonian connections and Athens' anti-Macedonian mood led to his being formally charged with impiety—the same charge leveled at Socrates. Allegedly claiming that he would not let the city sin twice against philosophy, he fled to Chalcis, where he died the following year.

Aristotle not only invented whole disciplines, he invented the very notion of a discipline as such

He produced an enormous body of work. Ancient commentators distinguish between his esoteric and exoteric writings—the former were highly technical pieces, written for use within the school, and the latter well-crafted pieces for public consumption. We know he wrote dialogues. We have Cicero's word that the public works were things of beauty, a "golden river of eloquence." No such work survives. We have only his technical, esoteric writings, and these are not beautiful in the usual sense, but are compact, crammed with jargon and what seem like technical preoccupations, stilted, and generally lacking in literary virtue. Actually, we have what are probably his lecture notes. They are works in progress, edited by those who came after, and discrepancies and inconsistencies sometimes confound us. Few, though, would be willing to trade even a scrap of it for a part of the public writings: though rough-going, Aristotle's surviving writings are crammed with the fruits of an incredible intellectual power.

The Rules of Logic

Aristotle more or less invented and formalized the rules of right reasoning, the beginnings of philosophical logic. He was the first to study the nature of deduction, to say what it means for a proposition to follow of necessity from premises, to identify and formalize different possible sorts of syllogism. With a general notion of proof in hand, he formalized the relation between the evidence gathered by studying things in the world and coming to true conclusions about those things. In doing this, he did much more than point us in the direction of what we now recognize as science. This alone would have been beyond impressive and earned him a large place in history, but his writings on logic and methodology constitute only a part of the Aristotelian corpus. Aristotle was just getting started when he invented science.

He wrote enormously influential treatises on ethics, politics, metaphysics, physics, mathematics, psychology, poetry, rhetoric, aesthetics, meteorology, geology, methodology, cosmology, philosophy of mind, theology, psychology, memory, and dreams, among much else. It is not going too far to say that he invented entire disciplines, whole regions of inquiry which still occupy us. More than this, Aristotle was the first to engage in the practice of distinguishing between different subject-matters; recapitulating and considering a topic's intellectual history; explicitly identifying the standards of evidence, degrees of precision, questions, and so on proper to each. Aristotle not only invented whole disciplines, he invented the very notion of a discipline as such.

All of this is to say nothing of his biological writings, which constitute perhaps a quarter of what we have. In a letter to William Ogle, a famous translator of Aristotle's biological works, Darwin mentions his "two gods" Linnaeus and Cuvier, concluding that they were "mere schoolboys to old Aristotle." It took a lot of thinking, nearly two thousand years of thinking, to get beyond Aristotle's teleological or goal-directed conception of life and the parts of animals. All of it follows from his famous four causes. The word "cause" is a little misleading, and one might just think of the four causes as the four explanatory features of a thing that we get by asking four sorts of question.

Questions of Nature

To use Aristotle's example, we might ask four questions about a statue: what is it made of (bronze: its material cause); what sort of thing is it (a statue: its formal cause); what brought it into being or initiated the changes that led to its being what it is (a sculptor: its efficient cause); and what is it for (decoration: its final cause). One gets a feeling from this that Aristotle is preoccupied with goals and ends, and it is true that Aristotle denies that we really know a thing, even a natural object or organ, until we know what it is for, what it aims at or does.

You will notice that Aristotle departs radically from Plato in this. Knowledge of this world is possible without recourse to a permanent realm of Forms. On the contrary, forms or universals exist only in the things in this world, and knowledge consists not in the contemplation of Forms, but in getting one's hands dirty, examining and dissecting and poking the things of this changing world, coming to know their causes. In the case of the statue and other artifacts, form is imposed by some outside agency; while in the case of natural objects, Aristotle argues, internal principles direct the thing such that it becomes what it naturally becomes.

Of those natural objects that live—plants, animals, and human beings—Aristotle's answer to the four questions of cause consists mainly in the activity of soul. The soul, for Aristotle, is not something ghostly that inhabits the body. Instead it is, at least in part, the distinctive functioning of the body in question; what initiates its movement fixes its aims. To oversimplify more than a little, a plant's soul is vegetative, and as such it consists in growing; an animal's soul consists in this plus movement, appetite, and the power to sense certain things; a human being's soul consists in this, plus the power to think and know.

The virtue, or excellence, of a thing for Aristotle consists in the full development of the distinctive potentialities latent in its particular nature. An excellent plant, then, is one that manifests the full flowering (literally) of the plant soul: it grows very well indeed. An excellent horse is one that realizes the potentialities of the distinctive movements of horses: it covers the ground; perhaps its quick eye and attentive ear contribute to its fleetness. Excellence or virtue for humans insofar as we are rational consists in action in accordance with reason. This, Aristotle famously claims, consists in choosing the mean.

Choosing the Mean

Virtue consists in choosing the mean between two extremes, that is, in feeling and acting rightly given all the peculiar circumstances of a situation. If one faces mortal danger, Aristotle argues that courage consists in choosing the mean between the excesses of foolhardy rashness on one side and cowardice on the other. When one speaks about oneself, the virtue of truthfulness consists in choosing the mean between boasting and undue modesty. It is clear that Aristotle is not advocating what one might mistake for a Christian ethic of unqualified moderation. The mean varies from person to person and situation to situation. For example, Milo the wrestler can choose his own mean when ordering the wine; an amount that is fine for him would be excessive for somebody else. There is nothing absolutist or exhaustive about Aristotle's notion of the mean: there is no mean when it comes to murder, he tells us. The best we can do is employ reason and decide on a case by case basis.

In what does the good life consist, given this view of virtue? Aristotle maintains that the good life requires friendship. Genuine virtue requires

MAJOR WORKS

We cannot say exactly when Aristotle wrote what has come down to us. It is likely that later editors made some changes and put the work in the order that it has now. Here is just some of it:

Nicomachean Ethics is among the most influential treatises on morality ever written. It contains a fascinating consideration of human happiness and virtue. It is perhaps most interesting for making the claim, forgotten by many later thinkers, that morality cannot be reduced to a series of universal principles.

Politics says something about the ideal state, which for Aristotle is one with the goal of well-being for its citizens. You will find here some disturbing remarks on slavery and the need for social harmony, which are partly mitigated by a consideration of the merits of democracy.

Physics is interesting for its consideration of the nature of explanation in what looks like budding science, as well as treatments of space and time. It also contains Aristotle's account of matter and form.

not only fellowship with equals, but sometimes self-sacrifice of varying sorts. Without friends, such action is not possible, and therefore a fully virtuous life is not possible. Friends afford the opportunity for goodness and happiness.

In addition, the full flowering of the intellectual virtues, the realization and exercise of our distinctive mental faculties, is required. Our rational capacities are part of what makes us what we are—just as a knife's capacity to cut makes a knife a knife. A good knife is one that cuts well, and a good human life is one filled with thinking well. A good life is certainly one in which we choose the mean, but it is also one in which rationality is given its head. Of the many goods we might aim at, the highest good, Aristotle argues, is the contemplative life, the life of the mind.

On with the Inquiry

This is, of course, only a caricature of the vast Aristotelian corpus. It overlooks many of the tensions, not to say outright contradictions, in his writing, and glosses over some very difficult technical philosophy. It is worth remembering, when we read him, that what we have really are works in progress, probably under constant revision throughout his life. It is difficult to imagine Aristotle satisfied with a treatise, content in the state of his own thinking on some matter or another, supposing, "Well, that's all there is to know about that." Aristotle was not so easily satisfied. Aristotle was also not one to waste last lines, and it is worth remembering the last line of the *Nicomachean Ethics* when faced with difficulties of interpretation. It is a long and bold treatise, dealing with more or less all thinking on ethics extant in Aristotle's time. He writes, at the end of what looks like a comprehensive account of virtue: "Come, let us get on with the inquiry."

Aristotle and his famous pupil. Aristotle tutored Alexander the Great for several years before Alexander became king of Macedonia.

Saint Thomas Aquinas

Saint Thomas Aquinas (1225/6–1274) was an Italian Catholic philosopher and a major figure—if not the major figure—in the scholastic tradition. He gave rise to the Thomistic school of philosophy, for a long while the primary philosophical mainstay of the Roman Catholic Church.

1225/6–74

The life of Thomas Aquinas ended in a manner not quite befitting a saint and a Dominican friar (the Dominican brotherhood places value on a life of poverty and undertakes the begging of alms). He was born in his family's castle, the youngest son of Count Landulf of Aquino and Donna Theodora, herself with connections to Norman nobility. His education began at the age of five, when he was sent to the Abbey of Monte Cassino, and continued at what would eventually become the University of Naples.

A Devout Youth

It was here that the teenaged Aquinas came under the influence of the Dominicans, and when his noble family discovered that their son was about to join the brotherhood, his scandalized mother dispatched his older brothers to Naples with orders to abduct him, the aim being to hold him until he saw reason. He was kept a prisoner in the family castle for over a year. On one occasion, his brothers sent a woman into his room in a last desperate effort to break his resolve. However, Aquinas chased her out with a burning stick from the fire. His family eventually despaired and relented. Aquinas won his freedom and joined the order.

...he produced a truly voluminous body of work—millions and millions of words

In 1252 he went to Paris and began to teach. Eventually he took a Chair in the Faculty of Theology of Paris University. He spent the rest of his life moving between learned institutions in Italy and France, throughout it all producing a truly voluminous body of work—millions and millions of words—all the more remarkable given his short life. He had as many as four secretaries taking dictation: because of his astonishingly large output, his allegedly appalling handwriting, or perhaps both. The torrent of words stopped abruptly, however, when he had what he took to be a religious experience during mass. "All that I have written seems to me like straw," he said, "compared to what has now been revealed to me." A few months later, en route to a church council, he was struck on the head by an overhanging branch. He died shortly thereafter.

His enormous output was partly the result of his intellectual power and partly because he lived in remarkably provocative times. The works of Aristotle had recently become available in the West again, sometimes with accompanying heretical but persuasive commentaries composed by non-Christian thinkers of the stature of Averroes. Here were nonbelievers, reasoning well, who came to conclusions apparently in conflict with Christian teaching. The soul, they argued, is not immortal; the universe was not begun by a single, divine creative act but exists eternally; God knows only himself, not us. While some, at the time, were content to show simply that Aristotle and his commentators must be wrong, Aquinas wrote twelve commentaries on Aristotelian doctrine, arguing that Aristotle was getting at something like the partial truth. It was not just an exercise by him in Christianizing Aristotle, but a necessary step to combat heretical thinking.

The Influence of Aristotle

It was Aristotle's methods, as much as his conclusions, that disturbed the scholars of Aquinas's time. Aristotle claims that one must recognize the difference between what is to be assumed and what is to be proven before thinking can get under way. Knowledge builds on itself, and some disciplines nearer the top of the edifice are dependent on the truths below; they get going with assumptions grounded elsewhere.

Nearer the foundations of the structure are truths every rational person just has to accept if he or she wants to be rational. You cannot play the rationality game and take part in a debate, for example, if you do not accept the Law of the Excluded Middle: there is nothing between the assertion and the denial of a proposition. Only "yes" or "no" count as answers to questions of the form: "Is it true that p?" If you do not accept that minimal requirement on rationality, you are doing something other than arguing; you have removed yourself from the debate. Assenting to some rules is just part of the warp and weft of rationality.

Aquinas draws a distinction between conclusions arrived at through reason and the truths of revelation. Obviously, the latter are authoritative for Aquinas, but (perhaps unusually for his time) he holds that the conclusions of reason in the writings of nonbelievers, Aristotle in particular, demand serious attention. Most interestingly, he argues that reason itself can arrive at some revelatory truths, and he sometimes adopts Aristotle's methods in order to do so. Further, his Dominican roots convinced him that one should stand ready to discourse on theology, particularly with those outside the faith. This means that premises must be sought to which even a nonbeliever would assent.

Perhaps this more than anything else explains the existence and tone of *Summa contra gentiles* (On the Truth of the Catholic Faith Against the Unbelievers). Next to his uncompleted masterwork, *Summa theologica* (Summation of theology), it is the best expression of his unusual attitude toward reason and those outside the faith.

Aquinas' Five Ways

An excellent example of Aquinas working with Aristotelian methods is to be found in his famous proofs of God's existence, the Five Ways or the *quinque viae*. Though their flavor might be owed to others, Aquinas's Aristotelian gloss makes his versions of the proofs remarkable. Each begins with empirical truths allegedly accepted by all and issues in the conclusion that God exists. We will consider just one, the Second Way.

Things in the world stand in causal relations. To use Aquinas's example, a stone moves, and this was caused by a stick that pushed it along, and this was caused by a hand, holding on to the stick, which moved it. Nothing, though, is a cause of itself; rather, causes are causes of other things, their distinct effects. An infinite regression of causal sequences is not possible. So there must be a first, uncaused cause, and this, Aquinas argues, everyone calls "God." In other words, one thing starts the whole chain going; one thing that is a cause but is not itself caused by anything else. Similar arguments are run for the existence of a first unmoved mover, a necessity underlying possibility; a perfection underpinning the gradations of the qualities of material things; and an argument for a God to explain the apparent order of the empirical world.

In each case, the argument runs backward from empirical facts accepted by all—facts of motion, causation, change, and qualities—to something responsible for the lot, something rendering intelligible the world around us. The arguments are open to many kinds of objection. One that most exercises philosophers takes issue with the move at the end of each argument, from the existence, say, of an uncaused first cause, to the existence of God: such and such must exist, and this we all call "God."

Why think that the uncaused cause has the many attributes we usually associate with the Christian God? Could there not be many uncaused causes at the back of the chain, rather than one God? Why think that the uncaused cause, if there is just one, is all-knowing, all-powerful, and all-good? Maybe it is a rather pedestrian uncaused cause: without much in the way of rationality, only just powerful enough to get things rolling, possibly with malice on its mind. There seems to be something missing, perhaps a premise, between the inference from whatever it is that underwrites the causal sequence to that thing's being God.

If Aquinas thinks that reason can tell us that God exists, he maintains that it cannot get nearly as far with regard to knowledge of the nature of God. While we are naturally equipped to come to know something of the physical world, our capacity to wonder about the nature of God outstrips our ability to understand. We come by such knowledge as we can get indirectly, by analogy and by negation, and Aquinas maintains that this knowledge is imperfect at best.

MAJOR WORKS

Written between 1261 and 1264, Aquinas's major work was **Summa Contra Gentiles** (On the Truth of the Catholic Faith Against the Unbelievers). It contains long treatises on the nature of God, creatures, the end (the purpose, or *telos*) of creatures, and revelation.

Unfinished at his death, **Summa Theologiae** (Summation of Theology) is an enormous work, running to sixty volumes. It contains detailed reflection and argumentation that continues to shape religious and philosophical thinking.

What We Can Know of God

A great deal of what we can say we know of God's nature results from negating the properties of material things which we know better. We can say that God is not anywhere, not any time, not changing, not finite, and so on. We can also come to a partial, imperfect understanding of God's attributes by analogy with our knowledge of some of our properties. God is perfectly good, and we can know something of this by reflecting on what we know of goodness. God wills, and while this is a different thing to human willing, we can have an imperfect grasp of it by analogy to human will.

Still, there are things Aquinas claims can be known about God's nature, though the story is a complex one. God's attributes are characterized by Aquinas as consisting in simplicity, actuality, perfection, goodness, infinitude, immutability, unity, and immanence. However, our access to this knowledge and the character of the knowledge itself are special. Aquinas argues that knowledge of the divine nature, beyond mere analogy and negation, is possible only in virtue of God's intervention—grace or the beatific vision. Where reason falters, revelation picks up the slack. We might be able to reason our way to the conclusion that there is a God, but only revelation can tell us, for example, that God is a Trinity. Finite beings as we are, though, even grace cannot convey a comprehension of the divine, only an apprehension.

Aquinas's Influence

It is worth noting that Western philosophy, not just Western theology, owes a debt to Aquinas. It is possible to get the impression that Aquinas's concerns were just to do with the existence and nature of God, but that would be a mistake. His vast writings include considerations of human nature, government, law, ethics, metaphysics, and epistemology, among a great deal else. In all of this Aquinas's influence has been large, both inside and outside the church.

Saint Thomas Aquinas standing between Aristotle and Plato and over the Arab philosopher Averroes. Detail from the Triumph of Saint Thomas Aquinas.

Niccolò Machiavelli

Born in Florence on May 3, 1469, Niccolò Machiavelli (1469–1527) is probably the world's best-known political scientist. His fame is such that his name functions as an adjective to denote cunning and unscrupulous behavior devised to attain a particular end.

1469–1527

To describe a politician as Machiavellian is to suggest that their lack of moral sensibility renders them unsuitable for public office. However, it is also to grant them a certain grudging respect, for Machiavellian behavior has come to be associated with a particular kind of cool, calculating intelligence.

Machiavelli first came to prominence as a young Florentine diplomat. He secured his position as head of the republic's second chancery in 1498, at the age of twenty-nine. At this time, it was the custom in Florence for people occupying government positions to have had a strong grounding in the humanities, and Machiavelli was no exception. His father, himself a keen scholar, had ensured that the young Niccolò received an education in the best traditions of Renaissance humanism.

This was something Machiavelli was never to forget—serious politics requires strength, fortitude, and the capacity to act decisively

The time that Machiavelli spent as a diplomat was essential to the development of his thought. Particularly, his ideas about effective leadership were rooted in a first-hand knowledge of the strengths and weaknesses of some of the major political figures of his age. Indeed, in his most famous work, *The Prince*, he made full use of a range of examples drawn from the real world, and in doing so, set himself apart from nearly all his predecessors. He was interested in the grubby world of day-to-day politics.

Diplomatic Education

The lessons Machiavelli learned as a diplomat began almost immediately. In 1500, he was dispatched to the court of Louis XII of France to discuss the problems that had occurred when Florence, despite help from France, had failed to subdue Pisa, a rebellious city-state which at one time had been under Florentine control. The mission was beset with problems from the start. Though Machiavelli had little respect for the King of France, he was shocked to discover just how little the French thought of Florence in return. His native city was considered feeble and irresolute, lacking both the military and financial power to make an impact in foreign affairs. This was something Machiavelli was never to forget; serious politics requires strength, fortitude, and the capacity to act quickly and decisively.

This was hammered home to him shortly afterward by the activities of Cesare Borgia, who notoriously employed a ruthless cunning to extend the scope of his power after he had been made Duke of Romagna by his father, Alexander VI. Machiavelli, who spent some time in the company of Borgia, clearly admired the way he dealt with his enemies. In *The Prince*, for example, he relates with approval how Borgia used deception in order to lure the leaders of the Orsini, a faction that had been plotting against him, to the town of Sinigaglia, where he promptly murdered them all. Machiavelli leaves us in no doubt that he thinks Borgia had many of the skills required for leadership:

> I believe I am correct in proposing that he be imitated by all those who have risen to power through Fortune and with the arms of others. Because he, possessing great courage and noble intentions could not have conducted himself in any other manner ... Anyone, therefore, who determines it necessary in his newly acquired principality to protect himself from his enemies, to win friends, to conquer either by force or by fraud, to make himself loved and feared by the people ... that person cannot find more recent examples than this man's deeds. (*The Prince*, Chapter 7)

Machiavelli's magnum opus The Prince *set out his notion of an ideal ruler.*

However, despite Borgia's undoubted talents, his power did not last long. Mainly this was a matter of bad luck, but Machiavelli does criticize him in *The Prince* for helping Cardinal Giuliano della Rovere to become Pope Julius II, even though he had every reason to suspect that Rovere would not be favorably inclined toward him once he gained the papacy. In Machiavelli's view, Borgia relied too heavily upon his own self-confidence and upon the continuation of the good fortune he had enjoyed earlier in his career. In the end, this was the cause of his downfall; political leaders need to be able to temper their personality in the face of the particular situations they confront, and ultimately Cesare Borgia was lacking in this ability.

Machiavelli's diplomatic career, while providing him with the experience that he was able to draw upon to write *The Prince*, came to an unfortunate end in 1512. He was dismissed from his post late that year after the Medici family, having come to power in Florence, dissolved the republic. To make matters worse, a few months later he was wrongly accused of plotting against the new Medicean government, and then tortured and imprisoned. It was out of this turn of events that he came to write *The Prince*.

NICOLAI
MACHIAVELLI
PRINCEPS.

EX
SYLVESTRI TELII
FVLGINATIS TRADVCTIONE
diligenter emendata.

Adiecta sunt eiusdem argumenti, Aliorum quorundam contra Machiauellum scripta de potestate & officio Principum, & contra tyrannos.

BASILEAE
Ex officina Petri Pernæ.
M D XXC.

After he was released, he needed a way to ingratiate himself with the new Medici rulers. *The Prince*, the book that secured his reputation, was an attempt to show that he had abilities and knowledge that might be useful to a new ruler. The book's dedication says it all: *Niccolò Machiavelli to Lorenzo de' Medici, the Magnificent.*

The Prince

The book is primarily an essay on the art of leadership. It was first published in 1532, some seven years after the death of Machiavelli, and it was initially well received. However, it fairly quickly gained a certain notoriety for its suggestion that leaders should set aside moral considerations when making political decisions. Indeed, Machiavelli is considered by many to be an amoralist; that is, to have no interest in whether leaders behave morally, only in whether they are able to secure and retain political power and glory.

There is certainly an element of truth in this characterization of Machiavelli's philosophy. For example, he completely rejects the traditional conception—as outlined in Cicero's *De Officiis*, for example—which holds that the rational person, in order to achieve honor and glory, will always choose to act virtuously:

> …there is such a gap between how one lives and how one ought to live that anyone who abandons what is done for what ought to be done learns his ruin rather than his preservation: for a man who wishes to make a vocation of being good at all times will come to ruin among so many who are not good. Hence it is necessary for a prince who wishes to maintain his position to learn how not to be good, and to use this knowledge or not to use it according to necessity. (*The Prince*, Chapter 15)

This idea that leaders must learn how not to be good in order to rule effectively is rooted in a jaundiced view of the nature of human beings. Machiavelli thought that people were "ungrateful, fickle, simulators and deceivers, avoiders of danger, greedy for gain" (*The Prince*, Chapter 17). As a result, certain styles of leadership just do not work. For example, Machiavelli argues that the prince who bases his power entirely on the love the people apparently have for him is likely to be deserted when the going gets tough:

> …men are less hesitant about harming someone who makes himself loved than one who makes himself feared because love is held together by a chain of obligation which, since men are a sorry lot, is broken on every occasion in which their own self-interest is concerned; but fear is held together by a dread of punishment which will never abandon you.

There is then something right about the accusation that Machiavelli's ideas about leadership are predicated on a certain kind of amorality. However, this is not the whole story, for it is also the case that Machiavelli thought that effective leadership would often have good outcomes for everybody. For example, when considering whether it is better for a prince to rule by mercy or cruelty, Machiavelli argued that the excessively merciful prince, by tolerating disorder, will often bring greater harm to a community than the cruel prince who creates harmony through fear. Similarly, he noted that generosity in a leader will almost inevitably result in discord among the populace, because in the end the prince who is predisposed to lavish displays of spending will have to tax the people in order to pay for them, and will be resented and disliked as a result.

The Measure of a Leader

There is also a more general way that Machiavelli avoids the charge of amoralism. It was his view that a leader should strive for the goals of honor and glory. Indeed, it is a measure of a prince's *Virtú* that he is willing to do whatever is necessary in the face of unpredictable fortune to achieve this end. However, in Machiavelli's eyes, this does not justify cruelty for cruelty's sake; such behavior might bring great power, but it will not bring honor and glory:

> Well used are those cruelties ... that are carried out in a single stroke, done out of necessity to protect oneself, and are not continued but instead converted into the greatest possible benefits for the subjects. Badly used are those cruelties which, although being few at the outset, grow with the passing of time instead of disappearing. (*The Prince*, Chapter 8)

Machiavelli's hope that *The Prince* would propel him back into public life did not come to anything. Indeed, shortly after its completion at the end of 1513, he came to recognize that his career as a diplomat was over, and increasingly he reinvented himself as a man of letters. In the remaining years of his life, he became more and more sympathetic to the case for republican government. Indeed, his most famous text of this period, *Discourses on the First Ten Books of Titus Levy*, is a defense of republican government which takes ancient Rome as its exemplary model. In many ways, *Discourses* is the most sophisticated of his works. However, it is not what Machiavelli is destined to be remembered for writing. Rather, history, in equal measure, celebrates and condemns Machiavelli as the man who claimed that leaders need the strength of a lion and the cunning of a fox.

MAJOR WORKS

Niccolò Machiavelli only published two significant philosophical works, *The Prince* and *The Discourses* (Discourses on the First Ten Books of Titus Livy). However, interested readers might wish to have a look at *Art of War*, and also his collected letters.

The Prince (1532)

Machiavelli's most famous work is an incisive analysis on the art of leadership. It is argued that it is the primary duty of political leaders to secure and maintain power; and that it is necessary for them to set aside moral considerations when pursuing strategies to this end. It is this book that bequeathed the term "Machiavellian" to posterity.

The Discourses (1531)

In some ways Machiavelli's most sophisticated work, *Discourses on the First Ten Books of Titus Livy*, is a defense of the principles of republican government, which takes ancient Rome as its exemplar.

Francis Bacon

Few philosophers divide the opinion of commentators as neatly as Bacon (1561–1626). Some have found early manifestations of the very precepts of the Enlightenment in his many writings, while others detect only anti-intellectual propaganda and a defense of the worst kind of religiosity.

1561–1626

Bacon is praised by some as the prophet of modern science, and identified by others as a buffoon whose only attempt at scientific experimentation resulted in his ridiculous death. He is currently reviled by ecofeminists for, among other things, his alleged view that Mother Nature is there to be tamed and dominated, and hailed by students of Karl Popper, who find in his writings deep insights into the nature of what would become scientific method.

His life also is plausibly viewed from two competing perspectives. From one vantage point, he is a philosopher with a brilliant legal mind who rose to the height of power before his enemies toppled him with trumped-up charges of corruption. From another he is an unscrupulous self-publicist and social climber, gaining advantage for himself by any means until he is finally and justly ruined by his own greed.

Well-Connected

He certainly was born with advantageous family connections, which he did try to use. His father was Sir Nicholas Bacon, Lord Keeper of the Great Seal of England, and his mother, Ann Cooke, was the sister-in-law of Sir William Cecil, Lord Treasurer. Following his education at Trinity College Cambridge, he was called to the bar and began a successful career in law. He combined this work with politics, joining Parliament at the age of twenty-three. He was befriended by the Earl of Essex, who tried to help him by loaning him money and by joining Sir William in lobbying for Bacon's advancement at court. You can imagine the Earl's dismay when Bacon later successfully prosecuted him for treason on the orders of Queen Elizabeth I. Despite Bacon's loyalty to the queen, if that's what it was, and perhaps because of some injudicious remarks made about the government's taxation policy in a parliamentary debate, Elizabeth chose not to advance him.

Bacon learned some sort of lesson from the queen's displeasure and did all he could to remain in favor with her successor, James Stuart. James sought the conviction of a prisoner and thought torture and confession the only way to secure it. Sir Edward Coke, Bacon's rival, demurred, but Bacon obtained the conviction as instructed. His advancement quickly followed. He was knighted, made Attorney General, Lord Keeper, Lord Chancellor, Baron, and finally Viscount St Albans. It is difficult not to wonder about the

Bacon saw in science nothing less than the possibility of understanding the natural world

hidden machinations responsible for Bacon's stellar promotion. It is this speculation that partly underpins the less charitable views of Bacon's life.

In the course of his career Bacon made enemies who eventually charged him with taking bribes. He admitted doing so, in some cases taking money from defendants in cases he judged, and the episode ruined him. He was fined the staggering sum of £40,000 and sent to the Tower. James eventually remitted the fine, released him from prison, and allowed him to retain his titles, but did not go so far as to pardon him officially. Bacon fled to the country but continued to write and reflect on both the law and science. In perhaps the most unfortunate death in the history of philosophy, the story goes that Bacon ventured outside on a cold winter's afternoon and stuffed a chicken's carcass with snow, perhaps experimenting with the notion that cold might preserve it. He contracted bronchitis and died soon after.

During the lean years, when Bacon was out of favor with Elizabeth, he wrote most of the fifty-eight essays for which he is duly remembered. The essays are entertaining and realist, perhaps Machiavellian—some contain advice to government officials on what we now recognize as spin-doctoring. However, it is *The Great Instauration*, the preface for six uncompleted works which together were intended to outline a program for the restoration and advancement of human knowledge, for which Bacon is most famous. When Bacon wrote it, natural philosophy or budding science was more than a little hit or miss. Practitioners sometimes undertook bizarre "experiments" simply to answer their own curiosity, and there was not much distinction between alchemy, magic, and embryonic scientific inquiry. Bacon saw in science, if it was properly understood and undertaken, nothing less than the possibility of understanding the natural world and, in so doing, becoming master of it.

Idols

In this work, Bacon identifies the most pernicious obstructions (false idols) that stand in the way of an objective study of nature: the idols of the tribe, idols of the cave, idols of the marketplace, and idols of the theater. In each are claims that still echo in the halls of philosophy departments.

MAJOR WORKS

Quite early on in his career, Francis Bacon had declared to the world that he would concern himself with "all knowledge." He then announced that he personally would carry out nothing less than the complete reform and reorganization of human thought.

Left unfinished at his death, **Magna Instauratio** or *Great Instauration* is Bacon's plan for this monumentally ambitious scheme.
Of the six parts of the work planned, only two were completed; the other four were left more as synopses than as any finished works.

De Dignitate et Augmentis Scientiarum (1623)
Part one of the Instauration, *Nine Books on the Dignity and Advancement of Learning*, was published in 1623. Essentially a redrafting of his earlier *Proficience and Advancement of Learning*, the work outlines what Bacon regards as the principle obstacles to learning.

Novum Organon or **New Tool (1620)**
Contains what Bacon takes to be the methods proper to the interrogation of nature as well as the so-called "idols" or impediments to truth.

The idols of the tribe are errors built into us as a species (the tribe of men). Humans see the world through human eyes, and such eyes are no sure guide to the real nature of things. Bacon has in mind not just the view that the senses are somehow fallible, but that humans are drawn into errors of judgment by an inbuilt, animal trust in sensory experience. Here too Bacon draws attention to something almost Kantian: that the mind imposes an order on what we see that is not really in the world. We are, Bacon argues, predisposed to order the world in our efforts to make sense of it, and in so doing we forget our active part in the order we find.

The idols of the cave are errors we are prone to as individuals, based on our particular preferences and agendas. What we notice in the world depends on our background of information: we notice what we are able to recognize and what interests us. One is no good in a dog-identifying contest if one doesn't much care about who wins, or has no idea what a dog is or looks like. Further, we overemphasize the importance of what we are looking for, what fits in with our aims or favorite prejudices, what slides easily along mental grooves long worn with use. Bacon's idea is that we are all imprisoned in our own theoretical frameworks, like the prisoners in Plato's cave, and can be misled by the dim reflections of our own view on things. We end up just preferring a certain familiar view of the world, and it blinds us to other possibilities. Bacon warns that whatever one "seizes on and dwells upon with peculiar satisfaction is to be held in suspicion."

The errors of the marketplace arise as a result of human interaction, and here Bacon is pointing to problems in language. He has in mind not just loose or ambiguous talk, but the human capacity to talk past another person, with both parties none the wiser. Further, the fact that a word exists for something does not bring that thing into existence, Bacon argues. No matter how much the philosophers might go on about the Prime Mover, we have no evidence for the existence of the thing in the bare fact of our language use.

Bacon's invective throughout this discussion, it seems, is reserved for the idols of the theater, and here he draws attention to the errors of traditional philosophical systems—no better than theatrical performances as guides to truth. While he takes issue with dogmatists who merely assert received philosophical opinion and the superstitious-minded who use philosophy to ground religion, his target is close to home: empirically minded philosophers whose methods Bacon hopes to correct. Conclusions based on too few experiments, limited observation, and general failures of classification and method stand in the way of an understanding of the world.

A New Method

His corrective is something more than mere enumerative induction, the practice of observing particular instances and inferring a general conclusion based on them. He writes:

> [T]he greatest change I introduce is in the form itself of induction and the judgement made thereby. For the induction of which the logician speaks, which proceeds by simple enumeration, is a puerile thing ... the greatest change I introduce is in the form of induction which shall analyze experience and take it to pieces, and by a due process of exclusion and rejection lead to an inevitable conclusion.

Bacon is advocating a methodical interrogation of natural phenomena in pursuit of more and more comprehensive laws, resulting in not just knowledge for its own sake, but power, utility, the control of things, and thus the improvement of human life. It is much more than particular observations issuing in a general conclusion.

Bacon viewed every natural object as an amalgam of a limited number of simple natures or properties. By careful experimentation, one identifies and lists the many circumstances in which all instances of a nature appear (Tables of Presence), all instances in which a nature does not appear (Tables of Absence), and all cases involving an increase or decrease in the presence of a nature in the same object (Tables of Degrees or Comparisons). Suppose you are investigating heat, to use Bacon's example. You might note its presence in boiling water, its absence in ice, and you might see that it decreases as boiling water cools.

On the basis of exhaustive studies of the presence and absence of natures and comparisons of their varying degrees, one is able to formulate axioms, interpretations, or what we would now recognize as hypotheses, which then guide the choices made in further tests. One has studied the presence and absence of heat in the various states of water, and on the basis of this, one might hypothesize that other liquids behave in a similar manner. What about mercury? The next step is to boil some mercury and continue recording the results. In due course, perhaps after boiling a lot of fluids, it is possible to formulate a general law, say, of the behavior of heat in liquids. The laws, Bacon argues, form a kind of pyramid of increasing coverage, and understanding and therefore control of things increases.

Of course, there might be a negative result, the hypothesis itself might be disproved, but this is still valuable. Bacon maintains that there are a limited number of natures and a limited number of false things to say about them. A negative result is in a sense better than a positive one. Discovering instances that support an hypothesis, even a very large number of instances, does not guarantee its truth. However, identifying falsehood amounts to a kind of certainty. True hypotheses have no false consequences, so a negative result is the only way to know for sure that a guess is the wrong one.

This is much more than the haphazard investigations that characterized "natural philosophy" in Bacon's time. This is recognizable science.

The title page of Bacon's Magna Instauratio, *showing a ship setting sail on a voyage of discovery across an ocean of knowledge, a metaphor later used by Isaac Newton.*

Thomas Hobbes

It is difficult to have anything but a great deal of admiration for someone who managed to annoy as diverse a group of people as did Thomas Hobbes (1588–1679).

1588–1679

English Parliamentarians were annoyed by his claim that the king's right to rule is absolute, and Monarchists by his suggestion that the root of this power is not divine but granted by the people. Hobbes annoyed mathematicians by insisting in the face of great criticism that he had squared the circle. He annoyed Descartes by offering profound objections to his views shortly before the publication of the *Meditations*. He annoyed at least one bishop with his position on free will and conducted a lifelong public and sometimes acrimonious debate with him on the subject. He annoyed the Church by arguing, among other things, that the king is in charge of the interpretation of Scripture and atheists by taking the sacrament when he mistakenly thought he was about to die. Proof that a lecturer had indulged in "Hobbism," a byword for atheism, was grounds for dismissal during Hobbes's lifetime. The possibility that Hobbes had annoyed even God was, for a time, seriously entertained.

Following the Great Fire of London and the Great Plague, Parliament wondered whether Hobbes's writings had provoked God's retribution and were somehow responsible for London's disasters. A committee was set up, which eventually demanded that Hobbes stop publishing.

Following the Great Fire and the Great Plague, Parliament wondered whether Hobbes's writings had provoked God's retribution

Hobbes did not annoy everyone, however. He counted among his friends and supporters Gassendi, William Cavendish, and at least one king. He was welcomed into the intellectual circle of the Abbé Mersenne, tutored English king Charles II, worked happily with Francis Bacon and exchanged views amicably with Galileo. And of course, he was concerned with more than just annoying people. He has been called, with some justice, the father of modern analytic philosophy, and he certainly ushered in modern political philosophy and social theory as we know it, breaking with traditional or mystical views of the origin of political power and turning instead to reason for its justification.

According to a story Hobbes himself did much to perpetuate, he was born prematurely when news of the approaching Spanish Armada frightened his mother into an early labor. His father was a vicar who fled the family home in some disgrace following his part in a brawl on the steps of his church. The young Hobbes was taken in by a well-to-do uncle, who saw to his education, eventually sending him to Oxford. Hobbes found lectures at university tedious, but following his

MAJOR WORKS

De Cive or On the Citizen (1642)

Perhaps the clearest and best articulated view of Hobbes' moral and political philosophy, despite the greater fame of *Leviathan*.

This book develops Hobbes' defense of the King's right to rule as an absolute monarch, first developed in *Elements of Law, Natural and Political* (1640).

Leviathan (1651)

Hobbes's philosophy undoubtedly finds its most complete expression in this work, his masterpiece of moral and political philosophy. The book begins with an avowedly materialistic account of human nature and knowledge, as well as a deterministic account of human volition and free will. Its most striking content, however, is the pessimistic vision of the natural state of human beings it provides. Hobbes regards this natural state as perpetual struggle against one's fellow man: it is in order to escape this grim fate, Hobbes argues, that we form the commonwealth, surrendering our individual rights to the authority of an absolute sovereign, who in return will ensure our security and well-being. For Hobbes, then, individual obedience to even an arbitrary government is necessary in order to forestall the greater evil of an endless state of war. The alternative to this commonwealth, Hobbes famously said, is a human life that is "solitary, poor, nasty, brutish, and short."

Leviathan also has an often neglected second half, which got Hobbes into trouble, concerning the philosophy of religion.

graduation, he had the great fortune of becoming tutor to the son of William Cavendish, which gave him the the use of a splendid library and the promise of travel.

During his travels in continental Europe, he discovered geometry and Galilean views on motion, and he put both at the heart of his thinking. Great strides could be made, he argued, by adopting a method owed to the proofs of geometry, that is, by beginning with small things and simple truths. Further, facts about human desire and sensation as well as large-scale human activities could be understood in terms of the motion of smaller parts. Laws not just of nature, but of human nature might be formulated. The bold culmination of Hobbes's thinking in this connection is *Leviathan*, which was published just after the execution of Charles I. When Hobbes returned from France, the powers in London were debating matters central to the book. Hobbes had a clearly articulated and highly relevant position, and his work was widely read.

Leviathan

The book is perhaps most famous for seeking a justification of political obligation through reflection on what human life would be without it, and Hobbes's conception of this state, the so-called "state of nature," reflects a kind of deep pessimism concerning what it is to be human. The state of nature is characterized by both liberty and equality of a distinctly dark sort. Everyone in the state of nature has a share in absolute liberty, which seems to have two parts: it entails both the freedom to have anything a person can possess and keep as well as the freedom to do anything he can to preserve himself and what he has. A person has the right, then, to take any action "to preserve his life" and "do what he would … to possess, use and enjoy all that he would, or could get." There is no such thing as a natural curb to human liberty, and Hobbes extends to the natural human even the right to kill. Further, everyone in the state of nature is also equal in power, in so far as anyone has the capacity to kill anyone else: even the weak can, quite literally, club together and collectively overcome the strong.

Thomas Hobbes' masterwork Leviathan. *The absolute ruler is shown watching benevolently over the land, armed with the badges of his authority, the sword and the scepter.*

People in the state of nature become enemies as surely as physical objects obey certain laws of motion. Goods, comforts, and resources are naturally limited or scarce, and so competition for them is intense. Equally intense is what Hobbes identifies as 'natural diffidence," which is the fear or insecurity that characterizes natural human life—there can be no trust in the state of nature. The natural condition of human beings, that is to say, ungoverned human beings, is war, "every man against every man." You would not enjoy life in the state of nature, but you could perhaps console yourself with the fact that your suffering would be short as you probably would not last very long. As Hobbes puts it, in the state of nature there is "no knowledge of the face of the earth; no account of time; no arts; no letters; no society; and which is worst of all, continual fear, and danger of violent death; and the life of man, solitary, poor, nasty, brutish, and short."

The Laws of Nature

But you would want things to change. Perhaps the single, dim ray of light in this otherwise dark conception of what it is to be human are the three laws of nature that Hobbes identified. These laws of nature are dictates of reason, or conclusions one in the state of nature simply must draw. The first and most obvious law is that one must desire and seek the peace. Rationality, coupled with the fear of death, requires that people must wish to get themselves out of the state of nature, achieve better lives and some measure of security. Like a geometrical proof, the other laws follow on from this.

If one must seek the peace, one is then obliged to give up a share of one's natural right, one's liberty. Peace is not possible if everyone has an equal share in liberty, an equal right to everything and the means simply to take it. So Hobbes' second law of nature is that everyone gives up this natural right and is "contented with so much liberty against other men, as he would allow other men against himself." This consists in a mutual agreement among all those who seek protection, that is, a social contract, which in effect transfers absolute liberty from everyone to a single person (or group) who is then charged with using this power to keep the peace and ensure the security of all. As Hobbes puts it: "… it is as if every man should say to every other, 'I authorize and give up my right of governing myself to this man or assembly of men, on this condition, that thou give up thy right to him, and authorize all his actions in like manner.'"

Hobbes's third law of nature is that people must keep their covenants. But this rational requirement might not be enough, Hobbes notes, as covenants "without the sword are but words." To ensure safety from the horrors of our natural state, a serious sword is required, and Hobbes takes it that the power of the sovereign must be unqualified. The only sure way out of the state of nature is complete submission to a single, absolute power. The social contract, then, brings into being "that great LEVIATHAN, or rather, to speak more reverently … that mortal God, to which we owe under the immortal God, our peace and defence."

It is worth noting an important fact about this set-up. It is the people themselves who contract together—the social contract is not entered into by the people on one hand and the ruler on the other. Instead, the people make a "free gift" of a part of their rights to the sovereign, and contract together to obey. Thus the king cannot in any sense break the contract, as he has not entered into it. However, reason demands that he avoid ingratitude, that he give the people no reason to "repent him of this gift." He is therefore obliged to make their safety the highest law. This might seem to you, rightly, as a thin restraint on the king and a thin basis for your protection. It has seemed to monarchists a little worrying too. Exactly what might happen should the people repent him of this gift? If the power of the sovereign rests on the consent of the governed, might that consent be lost or taken away?

The natural condition of human beings, that is to say, ungoverned human beings, is war, "every man against every man"

Criticisms of Hobbes

What seems to legitimize the absolute power of the government is the overwhelming desire to escape the state of nature. Hobbes's twin brother, fear, is at the heart of things here. Hobbes claims that reason leads us to the laws of nature, but it is fear of death and general insecurity that really warrant handing over liberty. It is worth asking whether fear really can lead us to the contemplation of not just someone who stands a chance of ensuring the peace, but a supreme and unlimited power. You might join John Locke in wondering whether this sort of thing is a good idea, even a rational course of action, for the fearful masses. If you fear even your fellows, can that fear be reason enough to create something monumentally dangerous? As Locke asks, a little incredulously, "Are men so foolish that they take care to avoid what mischiefs may be done them by polecats or foxes, but are content, nay think it safety, to be devoured by lions?" Even if we follow Hobbes some way in his thinking about political obligation, it is not clear that we should follow him to absolutism.

But many have followed Hobbes, at least part of the way, maintaining that political obligation depends on some sort of consent, and social contract theory now has a long history of defenders. Some now take the contract to be implicit, adopting the old Socratic argument that enjoying the comforts and protection of the state is enough to oblige you to obey it, or in other words that it is as good as signing a contract. The philosopher John Rawls tells a story not about the state of nature, but the original position, from which he derives various principles of liberty and equality which are certainly not absolutist in nature. One wonders whether Hobbes himself might have found this annoying.

René Descartes

René Descartes (1596–1650) is the author of perhaps the most famous philosophical quote of all, cogito ergo sum, *usually rendered as I think, therefore I am. There is, however, more to this quote, and to Descartes' philosophy, than meets the eye.*

1596–1650

René Descartes was reasonably young when burning astronomers seemed to the Church the right thing to do. Orthodox thinking at the time regarded the Earth as the center of the created order, with the heavenly bodies—all perfect spheres—tracing arcs around the Earth in divinely ordained, circular orbits. Not only did Galileo see through his telescope moons orbiting something else, namely Jupiter, but he observed too that at least some of the planets were not themselves perfect spheres: they were bumpy, irregular, maybe squashed. Some looked a bit cracked and pock-marked—not at all the kind of shoddy work one expects from the Creator. Despite the Church's warnings, Galileo pursued all of this in writing. He attracted the attention of the Inquisition, which forced his public recantation.

It is hard not to think that all of this had a large influence on Descartes. So too did his formal education among the Jesuits of the Collège de La Flèche, begun when he was just ten years old. The Jesuits promised clear and certain knowledge in return for diligent labor and careful study. As Descartes came of age, he found himself deeply troubled by uncertainty. He pouts: "… there was no such learning in the world as I had been led to hope." If Copernicus and Galileo were right, how could we have gone so spectacularly wrong in thinking about such large questions as where the Earth is or whether or not it moves or what the planets are doing? In the midst of such embarrassments, Descartes found a single and remarkable exception: mathematics. He was more than simply a mathematical genius or prodigy, and his successes in it convinced him that its methods might one day be employed to secure truth in all other disciplines.

The Copernican View

He presented a version of this thinking in his first major work, *Rules for the Direction of the Mind*, and made use of it in a large scientific treatise called *The World*. In the latter, Descartes joins Galileo in advocating a heliocentric, Copernican view of the solar system, as well as the notion that humans might aspire to a godlike understanding of the world. It was published in 1633, the very year in which Galileo was nearly destroyed by the Inquisition. Descartes heeded the lesson of Galileo's experience and suppressed his book himself.

Four years later, he published anonymously the parts of the book on geometry, optics, and meteorology, prefaced by what we now know as the *Discourse on Method*. It contains not only Descartes's rules for right reasoning in general but also the foundations of his epistemology and metaphysics. In a few short passages, Descartes breaks with more than a thousand years of thinking and ushers in the era of Modern Philosophy. The preoccupations, aims, and assumptions characteristic of the following three hundred years of philosophy are largely those of Descartes.

The method is a generalization of Descartes's conception of mathematical demonstration. Even the most complex mathematical proofs are accomplished by a series of smaller steps—the truth of each, as well as nearby connections, are easily grasped. So too, Descartes argues, for all rational inquiry. Descartes encapsulates his method in four rules. (1) Accept nothing as true that is not presented to the mind so clearly and distinctly that there is no reason to doubt it. (2) Break problems down into as many smaller problems as possible. (3) Begin with what is most simple and easily understood, and build on this by degrees to larger and more complex matters. (4) Review the entire chain of thinking to ensure nothing is omitted.

Doubt and Knowledge

The first rule is probably the best known, as it is boldly expressed in the opening paragraphs of Descartes's *Meditations on First Philosophy*, perhaps the most important book of the modern period. Descartes hopes to secure a firm foundation for the natural sciences by establishing a first truth or truths. He does so by rejecting any beliefs that are open to even the slightest doubt, in the hope that at least one belief will survive and serve as a basis for further truths. The conception of knowledge operative here and in his other writings depends on a strict relation between knowing and certainty. If one genuinely knows some proposition, there is no room at all for doubt. Knowing requires certainty. Therefore, while the skeptical arguments of the first meditation might seem unpersuasive to one in a casual frame of mind, do note that Descartes is in pursuit of certain truth. If he finds even the slightest reason to doubt some belief or other—the most outlandish reason will do—the belief is no candidate for the firm foundation he seeks.

Descartes first notes that the senses can be deceptive, for instance, when one sees a stick that appears bent in a stream, and a wise person never trusts that which once deceives him. Ought we therefore never trust our sense-based beliefs? The argument cannot prove this much, not least because we would not be aware of illusions if we had no faith at all in sensory perception. We discover that the stick is not really bent by calling on the reinforcements of other sensory experiences; we feel the stick or take it out

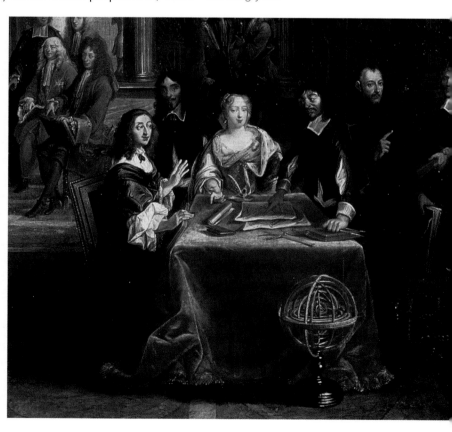

Descartes conducts a demonstration at the court of Queen Christina of Sweden, where he became "philosopher-in-residence" in 1649 until his death the following year.

of the water and look at it again. Descartes acknowledges this, saying that it would be a little crazy to think, just on the basis of the odd illusion, that he was not seated by the fire right now, writing in his notebook.

The second argument undercuts even this sort of everyday belief: one might be dreaming that one sees what one sees. Dreams, at the time of dreaming anyway, can seem just like waking life. If we have no criterion by which to distinguish being awake from being asleep, how do we know that for any belief we take to be true, we might not have dreamed its truth? Maybe your belief that your hand is holding this book is false. Actually, you are sound asleep, your eyes are closed, and your hand is under the pillow. The trouble here is that for any alleged criterion for wakefulness, we can imagine the possibility of dreaming its satisfaction: you might dream of pinching yourself or waking up and realizing you were dreaming, and so on. Descartes argues that the dreaming possibility proves quite a bit. It casts doubt on all beliefs that require the world to be a certain way, and leaves us with only belief in the most simple and universal things: facts about bodies and shapes in general, place and time, and the truths of mathematics and logic.

I think, therefore I am

These remaining beliefs are rendered dubious by certain reflections on our origins. We might have been created deliberately by God, who is certainly powerful enough to have built us to go wrong even with regard to simple and universal things, say something as obvious as counting the sides of a square. (If the possibility of a deceptive God is too heretical for you, Descartes offers the possibility of a malicious demon bent on your confusion.) Or we owe our existence to a sequence of accidental causes, in which case it is all the more likely that we are imperfectly built and again might go wrong with respect to even the most simple and universal things. The first meditation ends with Descartes contemplating the possibility that all his former beliefs are open to doubt.

Cartesian Dualism

It turns out, though, that one resilient belief remains. If deluded by illusion, led astray by a dream, or deceived by a demon, Descartes nevertheless cannot doubt that he himself exists. This is the first certainty of the *Meditations*, the anchor or foundation on which the Cartesian project depends: "[T]his proposition 'I am,' 'I exist,' whenever I utter it or conceive it in my mind, is necessarily true." The Latin for this discovery, *Cogito ergo sum* (I am thinking, therefore I exist), is perhaps the best-known philosophical catchphrase ever formulated. It is on the basis of the Cogito, as this first certainty is sometimes called, and in accord with his method, that Descartes attempts to build a series of additional truths.

The certainty, though, is a bare one. By "I," Descartes means only a thing that thinks—that doubts, affirms, seems to see, hopes, and so on. His bodily nature and bodies in general remain open to doubt. This epistemological distinction is transformed by Descartes into a shaky metaphysical one, Cartesian Dualism: the mind and body are distinct things, different kinds of substances. Minds are things that think, and bodies are extended things, space-occupiers. The argument for the distinction depends on conceivability: it is conceivable that the mind can exist without the body; it is therefore possible that the mind can exist without the body; if such a thing is possible, then the mind and body cannot be the same thing. But of course conceivability is no sure guide to possibility. What we can conceive of depends on our background of theory and experience; it tells us something about our concepts but nothing clearly follows about the way the world is.

The distinction faces other problems too, perhaps the most difficult of which is the problem of interaction: exactly how can a thinking substance, which Descartes claims is not located in space, stand in a causal relation to a body, a thing that is located in space? This is a version of the mind-body problem, and modern philosophy of mind might be viewed as an attempt to struggle free of the concepts of mind and body that Descartes has bequeathed to us. We have not yet managed it. We have many new distinctions and formulations of the problem—we have even contemplated some uncomfortable solutions—but it would be very optimistic to say that we are much closer to the solution than was René Descartes.

Whatever we make of dualism, Descartes follows the Cogito with further reflections, careful to assent only to that which is clearly and distinctly perceived, noting in particular the idea of a perfect God resident among the contents of his mind. Arguing that an effect must have at least as much reality or perfection as its cause, he claims that he could not simply have invented the idea of God. So Descartes is led to the belief that God exists and a conception of God as both a creator and a being without defect. Being deceptive is a kind of defect, and so Descartes reasons that God is no deceiver. If God is no deceiver, then we are not systematically misled with respect to those things we clearly and distinctly perceive, beliefs that survive our best and most careful scrutiny. It is a short step from here to the recovery of certain beliefs about the external world.

You might have noticed a tight circle in this series of reflections. God's goodness ensures that our clear and distinct perceptions are true; the proof of God's existence depends on such clear and distinct perceptions. The trouble is part of Descartes's legacy to us: beliefs seem easy to undermine but impossible to restore. Most commentators agree that Descartes's negative project of belief destruction succeeds, but his positive efforts to restore a firm foundation fail. Contemporary epistemology is, in large measure, an attempt to exorcise Descartes's demon.

MAJOR WORKS

Le Monde (1633) defends a heliocentric view of the solar system, and Descartes suppressed it himself, fearing censure by the Church.

Discourse on Method (1637) is the preface to *Optics, Meteorology and Geometry*, a toned-down version of *Le Monde*. It is this preface that largely shaped modern philosophy, breaking as it did with Bacon's notion of scientific inquiry as well as Aristotelian thinking.

Meditations on First Philosophy (1641) might be the Modern Period's most important book. Certainly it put epistemology at the center of philosophy and left us with skeptical problems we still deal with today. It lumbered us with Cartesian Dualism, the view that mind and body are distinct substances. It is also, of course, of interest to philosophers of religion for both Descartes' proof of God's existence and the role Descartes assigns to God in our efforts to understand the world.

Principles of Philosophy (1644) partly restates the metaphysical conclusions of the *Meditations*, focusing in particular on the relation of body and soul, but it also contains new material on the structure of the universe.

John Locke

John Locke (1632–1704) concerned himself primarily with society, where his views are often contrasted with those of Thomas Hobbes, and epistemology, where he is usually put with David Hume and Bishop Berkeley into the group known as the British Empiricists.

1632–1704

It is widely agreed that John Locke (1632–1704) is the father of modern empiricism, the view that knowledge comes not from innate ideas but from experience. He is also undoubtedly a vastly influential moral and political philosopher, and some would go so far as to say that his thinking made possible the revolutions in both America and France. It is hard not to think of him as the greatest philosopher of the modern period in England—he did much to disentangle the philosophy of his day from scholastic and ancient Greek thinking. Some are willing to go further, arguing that he is the greatest philosopher England has ever produced. Certainly he shares a property with many others at the very top of the pantheon: those in power put him in fear for his life at least once.

Locke was born in Wrington, Somerset, England, to stern parents of the Puritan faith. His father arranged for his early education at Westminster School in London, where he eventually boarded, finally leaving to take up a studentship at Christ Church, Oxford, in 1652. It was at Christ Church that Locke began the odd practice of writing in codes and using invisible ink to keep his work secret. Many of Locke's papers and books were first published anonymously, and he seems to have been extremely secretive and suspicious of certain apparently blameless friends throughout his life.

Political Upheavals

Locke was much taken by the successes and the observational methods of what was then the new science, no doubt influenced by his colleague and friend at Oxford, Robert Boyle. His greatest friend at this time was Baron Ashley, who was eventually the Earl of Shaftesbury, who took such a liking to him that he made Locke his personal physician and quartered him in his London home. Locke assisted the Earl in a number of ways, and his friend seems to have had him appointed to several public boards. He became secretary to the Council of Trade and Plantations, which by all accounts he handled admirably and efficiently—he would eventually become its Commissioner. Locke was getting on well in the world.

His fortunes changed, however, when his patron became one of the leaders of parliamentary opposition to the Stuarts. Shaftesbury was tried and acquitted of treason in 1681, but, given his close association, Locke feared that he might be in danger too. He was right. Locke fled to Holland in 1683, and James II insisted that the Dutch return him to

England, possibly to be tried as a traitor. Little was made of this demand in Holland, but Locke was nevertheless forced to hide with supporters for a time. If his decade-long exile was sometimes harrowing, it nevertheless afforded Locke both the time and the intellectual stimulation he required to focus on two books he had been writing intermittently for perhaps a decade. By 1687, Locke was among the advisors of William of Orange, and when William was finally crowned, Locke returned, escorting the future Queen Mary. He was offered and took a number of posts, but devoted at least some of his time to completing his books.

Two Treatises of Government

One of these books, *Two Treatises of Government*, sets out Locke's political philosophy, and it is certainly a product of his times. The first treatise is an attack on the very idea of the divine right of kings, but it is the second that is most widely read. In it Locke argues that people living without a civil government in an imagined state of nature have certain duties to God not to harm the body, property, or liberty of another, as well as corresponding rights to defend themselves, their property, and their liberty. In contrast to Hobbes's claim that only an absolute ruler can save a person in the state of nature from the brutality of others, Locke argues that people form a government as a matter of convenience, designating a judge or set of judges to defend their natural rights. Although reason dictates that certain laws must be obeyed, not everyone has an equal share in rationality, and anyway it is possible for people to have reasonable disagreements. What is needed is a disinterested judge or set of judges, and this is the principle motivation for political obligation, for the social contract itself. In further contrast to Hobbes, the social contract is between the people and their appointed or otherwise chosen defenders. This makes possible a kind of contractual set of duties on the part of both the government and the people, and it has large implications. In virtue of their tyrannical conduct, for example, those in power might warrant their own overthrow.

In contrast to Hobbes, Locke argues that people form a government as a matter of convenience

Concerning Human Understanding

The other book is *An Essay Concerning Human Understanding*, which Locke claims was inspired by a perplexing discussion he had with some friends while in the service of Shaftesbury—according to one source who probably was there, the topic was morality and revelation. They found themselves unable to make any headway and concluded that before progress could be made "it was necessary to examine our own abilities, and see what objects our understandings were or were not fitted to deal with." At the heart of this inquiry is the notion of an idea, because for Locke an idea is "whatsoever is the object of the understanding when a man thinks." What our minds are fitted to deal with depends on the nature of our ideas, and for Locke this question turns on how our ideas actually arise.

The first book of the *Essay* is an extended argument against the possibility that ideas are innate. This doctrine consists in the claim that the mind contains at least some ideas or principles that are not delivered by experience: some ideas are simply part of our factory specification. The view is first clearly expressed in Plato's thinking, but it is evidently

John Locke

accepted by many of the schoolmen, as well as both Descartes and, with some qualifications, Leibniz in the modern period. Locke almost single-handedly derails this line of thinking.

The Doctrine of Innate Ideas

Locke takes it that the doctrine of innate ideas implies that there must be ideas or principles assented to by everyone, and he argues that there is no such universal assent. To use Locke's example, even a rock-bottom logical principle apparently required for reason to get off the ground is not assented to universally. "Whatsoever is, is" might be such a principle, but the principle is not even known, let alone assented to, by "children and idiots."

It might be replied that anyone who is able to employ reason, or, in the case of a child, anyone who eventually comes to reason, will assent to such principles, and this proves that the principles are themselves innate, imprinted on the mind, waiting for discovery. Locke argues that this is no proof of innate ideas. First of all, it proves too much: it makes anything reason discovers, even truths of mathematics, innate. Second, even if everyone assents to some principle or other on coming to reason, this does not prove that the principle is innate. Another explanation or view of the origin of ideas fits this bill too. It is Locke's formulation of empiricism, his account of the opposing view, that is perhaps the best argument against the notion that some ideas are innate.

Locke argues that we are born with minds like blank tablets (*tabula rasa*), and experience alone is the source of our ideas. Ideas of sensation issue from our sensory experience, when our sensory apparatuses come into contact with the world, while ideas of reflection result from introspection, when we note the operations of our minds on ideas acquired by sensation. Ideas, considered generally, are of two types: simple and complex. A simple idea is "nothing but one uniform appearance or conception in the mind, and is not distinguishable into different ideas." Complex ideas are themselves composed of

William of Orange, the future William III of England, was Locke's patron during his years in exile in the Netherlands.

simple ideas. The mind is incapable of generating simple ideas, but it can furnish itself with complex ones by combining and shifting its store of simple ideas.

Primary and Secondary Qualities

It is easy to wonder about the relation between our ideas, the objects of knowledge according to Locke, and the real things in the world. Here Locke introduces a second distinction between the primary and secondary properties of objects. The former are "utterly inseparable" from material objects; remain the same throughout all changes; and are a part of "every particle of matter." Locke identifies solidity, extension, figure, bulk, and motion as primary properties of objects. Secondary properties, however, are "nothing in the objects themselves but powers to produce various sensations in us by their primary qualities." Here Locke has in mind colors, tastes, touches, smells, and sounds. Our idea, say, of the shape of a lemon really does tell us something about the way the world is, but not so, or not exactly so, with the taste of a lemon.

Both the distinction between simple and complex ideas and the distinction between primary and secondary qualities have large implications for the limits of human understanding. At the end of the *Essay*, Locke's consideration of true and false ideas more or less outlines these limits from the empiricist point of view, and the fallout from his conclusions has been extensive. Locke maintains, for example, that there is a sense in which our complex ideas can lead us astray. We might combine simple ideas in such a way that nothing in nature answers to them. Hume argues that this is the case with such philosophical fictions as the enduring self, necessary causal connections, and external objects—all are ideas that seem to lack a corresponding and legitimizing sensory impression. There also arises the question of the relation between our ideas of the qualities of objects and those objects themselves, a question pressed home by Berkeley. Locke's distinction between primary and secondary qualities requires that at least some of our ideas do not represent the way the world really is. It is a short step from here to wondering whether any of our ideas do.

Locke's Influence

Locke was much troubled in his lifetime by critics who thought that his empiricism could lead only to skepticism. However, with hindsight, we know that Locke's work led to much more. His thinking made not just Hume and Berkeley possible, perhaps even inevitable, but Kant and the tradition that followed him, not to mention the many manifestations of empiricism both within and without philosophy ever since. Locke's influence is evident most recently in the work of the pragmatists, the logical positivists, and those those who argue that philosophy ought to be informed by the empirical sciences, philosophers who are hard at work in the present day.

MAJOR WORKS

Two Treatises of Government (1690) contains Locke's best political writing. The first treatise gives an account of Locke's critique of the divine right of kings. The second proposes Locke's alternative, the view that political obligation consists in the consent of the governed.

An Essay Concerning Human Understanding (1690) is Locke's greatest philosophical achievement. His aim in it is to determine exactly what the human mind is fitted to understand, and the book contains considerations of knowledge of the self, the world, and God. The book might be best known for Locke's annihilation of the doctrine of innate ideas. It gave empiricism a new start in the seventeenth century.

Baruch Spinoza

Baruch Spinoza (1632–77) has inspired much admiration and affection from philosophers and students of philosophy alike: Bertrand Russell said of him that he was "the noblest and most lovable of the great philosophers."

1632–77

This did not, however, as Russell went on to note, preclude Spinoza from being reviled in his time for his religious heterodoxy; indeed, as a young man he was excommunicated from his Jewish community for "horrendous heresies." The cause of his troubles were the unorthodox beliefs he held about God and the universe.

Spinoza was born in Amsterdam on November 24, 1632. His family were crypto-Jews; that is, they had been forced to adopt Christianity, yet secretly maintained their Jewish faith. His father, a successful merchant, had emigrated to Amsterdam in order to avoid persecution, and occupied a position of some prominence in the Jewish community. The young Spinoza was educated at the local Jewish school and synagogue, where he learnt Hebrew and Jewish theology. Outside school hours, he was tutored in Latin, German, and some of the other European languages. Spinoza's father hoped that his son would choose to become a rabbi. However, by the time Spinoza turned twenty, it was clear that this was not going to happen.

A Path from Judaism

Under the influence of Frances van den Enden, a private tutor, Spinoza had become increasingly dissatisfied with his rabbinical teachers, and had begun to identify with a number of unorthodox Christian groups, including, most significantly, the Collegiant sect. All this had placed his relations with the wider Jewish community under strain. Things came to a head in 1653, when he refused to repent his opinion that there is nothing in the Bible to lead one to suppose that God is without a body. After a thirty-day period of excommunication, he was cursed and thrown out of the synagogue for good. On being informed of his fate, he reportedly replied: 'Very well. This does not force me to do anything that I would not have done of my own accord, had I not been afraid of a scandal."

Given his treatment at the hands of religious authority, it is surely no coincidence that one of the two books he published in his lifetime was a call for religious tolerance and freedom. Published anonymously in 1670, the *Tractatus Theologico-Politicus* treated the Bible as a historical, culturally embedded document, which inevitably reflected the limited understanding of its authors. Thus, for example, Spinoza denied that the biblical miracles were supernatural in origin, claiming rather that they were natural phenomena which had been misunderstood by the authors of the Bible because of a lack of knowledge. Spinoza did, however, believe that the Bible articulated a consistent moral vision—one based on a message of love—and that it contained nothing to suggest that it supported religious intolerance.

Spinoza's *Ethics*

There is a certain irony in Spinoza's troubles with religious authority because it was his belief that God is literally everywhere. Or, to put this more accurately, it was Spinoza's claim that every existing thing is an aspect of just one substance, which is accurately described as God or Nature. He set out this view in his most famous work, *Ethics*, which was published by his friends shortly after his death.

The *Ethics* is a difficult read. This is partly because of the way in which it is constructed. Spinoza sets it down in a geometrical style, with rigorous, deductive argumentation from premises to conclusions. Indeed, according to Bertrand Russell, it is not worth the while for a modern student to learn the details of Spinoza's technical argument; it is enough to concentrate on the less formal remarks that appear in the notes and appendices.

Human beings themselves do not have a separate reality; they are simply aspects of the infinity of God

Despite its difficulties, however, the *Ethics* is undoubtedly one of the classic texts of Western philosophy, so it is worth having a look at some of its arguments. In the first part of the work, Spinoza set out his metaphysical ideas, which rest on the notion that reality comprises just one substance—which, as indicated above, can be conceived of as either God or Nature. Spinoza argued that this one substance has an infinite number of attributes; however, it is only possible for human beings to know two of them, physical extension and thought. Human beings themselves do not have a separate reality; they are simply aspects of the infinity of God.

Immediately, it is possible to see how Spinoza's views came to be seen as heretical: God did not create nature, but rather God is equivalent to nature; and human beings are not straightforwardly the subjects of God, but rather aspects of God. Moreover, Spinoza's view had implications for some of the standard themes of Christian

MAJOR WORKS

Baruch Spinoza only published one major work in his lifetime (*Theological-Political Treatise*). His outstanding work, *Ethics Demonstrated in a Geometrical Manner* (The Ethics), although completed in 1675, was not published until shortly after his death.

Theological-Political Treatise (1670)

This work treats the Bible as a historical, culturally embedded document, which inevitably reflects the limited understanding of its authors. The book was published anonymously as Spinoza was concerned, not without reason, as to the sort of reception it could expect from organized religion.

The Ethics (1677)

Spinoza's major work, indeed one of the classics of modern philosophy, in which he sets out his metaphysical ideas, which rest on the notion that reality comprises just one substance, which can be conceived of as either God or Nature. *Ethics* was not published during Spinoza's lifetime, partly at least because he feared the reaction its publication would provoke.

theology. Perhaps most significantly, his idea that everything that occurs is simply a necessary manifestation of God or Nature allowed no room for free will, and consequently it rendered the notion of sin moot at best.

Spinoza was fully aware of this implication of his work. He claimed that people who believe "that they speak or keep silence or act in any way from the free decision of their mind, do but dream with their eyes open"; and it is only because they are ignorant of the true causes of their actions that they are able to hold on to their dream:

> Experience teaches us no less clearly than reason, that men believe themselves to be free, simply because they are conscious of their actions, and unconscious of the causes whereby those actions are determined; and, further, it is plain that the dictates of the mind are but another name for the appetites, and therefore vary according to the varying state of the body. (*Ethics*)

Implications of the *Ethics*

The implications for ideas to do with sin and damnation are clear. If nothing can be other than it is, then what of moral responsibility? If the murderer has no freedom to choose not to murder, then it isn't clear he is morally responsible for his actions. And if everything in the universe is an aspect of God, then how can anything be bad or wrong? Interestingly, Spinoza's response to this question anticipated Leibniz's treatment of the problem of evil. He argued that when viewed from the point of view of God, there is no evil in sin, since from the perspective of the totality there is nothing negative in sin; human beings only see evil in the world because they are unable to see how the whole of reality fits together. In other words, like Leibniz, he thought that our understanding of evil is distorted by our ignorance of the Divine.

However, it would not be true to think that Spinoza's system has no implications for the way that people should live. It was Spinoza's belief that the task for human beings is to see reality as God sees it, that is, from the perspective of eternity, or, in his words, "under the aspect of eternity" (*sub specie aeternitatis*). To the extent that we are able to achieve this, we gain a kind of freedom; by recognizing our place in the larger whole and seeing its goodness, we free ourselves from certain of our passions, particularly those rooted in hopes and fears that are predicated upon human finitude. Thus, for example, Spinoza claimed, "A free man thinks of nothing less than of death; and his wisdom is a meditation not of death, but of life."

It should be clear why the arguments set out in the *Ethics* were unacceptable in terms of the orthodox Christianity of Spinoza's day. They were clearly contrary to many of the central tenets of the Christian faith, including, for example, the idea of the Fall of Man, the possibility of salvation and everlasting life through an acceptance of Jesus Christ, and the notion of God as the Father of Man.

Spinoza was well aware that the publication of his great work would earn him the opprobrium of the religious establishment. In fact, this occurred even without its publication, as he wrote to Henry Oldenburg, secretary of the Royal Society:

[A] rumor gained currency that I had in the press a book concerning God, wherein I endeavored to show that there is no God. Hence certain theologians, perhaps the authors of the rumor, took occasion to complain of me before the prince and magistrates … When I became aware of this through trustworthy men, who also assured me that the theologians were everywhere lying in wait for me, I determined to put off publishing till I saw how things were going …

In fact, the book was not ever published in his lifetime. In 1676, Spinoza began to experience health difficulties; he had, for a while, been suffering from tuberculosis, which likely had been made worse by his work as a lens grinder. He died on February 21, 1676 at the age of forty-three. His biographers report that he met his death as his philosophy commanded, calmly and without complaint.

Spinoza enjoys a somewhat paradoxical reputation among philosophers today. His *Ethics* is recognized as one of the great achievements of Western philosophy, yet it is rarely studied in detail. This is perhaps because his metaphysics has largely been discounted; pantheism, the notion that God is in everything, has always been a marginal belief, and when it is combined with a smidgen of panpsychism—roughly speaking, the idea that mind is everywhere—it becomes even more marginal. However, Spinoza's ethical ideas retain their pertinence; particularly, there is something to be said for considering the travails of humanity from the perspective of the whole of reality; not in order to lessen our moral sensibility, but rather to help us to understand that we are but a tiny part of the universe. Bertrand Russell, in his great history of Western philosophy, suggested that in a painful world such reflections "are a help towards sanity and an antidote to the paralysis of utter despair." If he is right, then Spinoza's philosophy has something to teach us even today.

Moses parts the Red Sea and allows the Jews to escape their Egyptian pursuers. According to Spinoza, miracles such as this were no more than natural phenomena, a view that did little to endear him to Orthodox Judaism.

Gottfried Leibniz

Gottfried Leibniz (1647–1716), among his other achievements, invented differential calculus independently of Isaac Newton; much of the notation and vocabulary used today comes from Leibniz, who possessed a flair for both symbolism and language. He was also a pioneer in the field of symbolic logic.

1646–1716

My opinion is that God does nothing for which he does not deserve to be glorified

However, it is the misfortune of Leibniz that he is probably best known to most people as the inspiration for Dr Pangloss, the satirical creation of the French philosopher Voltaire, who spends his time in the novel *Candide* insisting that all is for the best in the best of all possible worlds, despite the fact that he is confronted with disaster after disaster. There is an element of truth in this characterization of Leibniz's philosophy—or his metaphysico-theologo-cosmolonigology, as Voltaire put it—but it would be a mistake to think that Leibniz was some sort of buffoon, since, in fact, he was one of the leading intellectual figures of his age.

He was born in Leipzig on June 21, 1646. His father, who taught Moral Philosophy at the University of Leipzig, died when he was only six years old, and he was raised mainly by his mother, who was careful to nurture and encourage his precocious intellectual talents. He taught himself Latin at an early age in order to read Livy, and then, having been given free run of his father's library, worked his way systematically through the ancients, Cicero, Herodotus, Seneca and Plato.

Leibniz went off to university when he was only fifteen years old, first to Leipzig and then to Altdorf, graduating with degrees in Law and Philosophy. After receiving his doctorate in 1667, he was offered a professorship, but he declined it in favor of a diplomatic position at the Court of the Elector of Mainz. This decision was crucial to his intellectual development. In 1672, he was sent on diplomatic business to Paris, where he remained for four years, during which time he began to establish his reputation in European intellectual circles, meeting some of the leading thinkers of his day, including the mathematician Huygens, and the theologian and philosopher Malebranche.

During his time in Paris, Leibniz showed that he had wide intellectual interests. It was during this period that he laid down the foundations of differential calculus—independently of Newton—an achievement which would have recommended him to posterity even if he had done no important work in philosophy. He possessed prodigious ability in a number of separate fields. Like the French philosopher and mathematician Blaise Pascal, he invented a calculating machine; he also designed various wind- and water-powered pumps that were supposed to drain mines (unfortunately, they didn't!); and he did significant work in geology, physics, and even history.

Possibly because of his wide range of interests, his philosophy was never laid down in systematic fashion. Indeed, he only published one book in his lifetime—*The Theodicy*—preferring instead to set down his philosophy across a series of short articles and in voluminous correspondence. It is, nevertheless, possible to identify a number of key themes in his work.

The Best of all Possible Worlds

Perhaps the most important of these is the philosophical optimism that Voltaire satirizes in *Candide*. According to Leibniz, this world is the best of all possible worlds; to our modern minds—and, indeed, to Voltaire's not so modern mind—this is a somewhat implausible idea, but Leibniz thought it could be deduced from the terms of a rationalist theology. Put simply, the ontological argument shows that God, the most perfect being, exists; since he is perfect, it is inconceivable that he might have made things better than he has; therefore, this world is the best of all possible worlds.

Needless to say, this line of reasoning immediately raises a whole series of further issues. Even leaving aside questions about the ontological proof, there are problems with the argument. For example, it is possible that there is no best world, in which case God can only choose from an infinite series of worlds where each is better than the last. Leibniz rejects this criticism on the grounds that it compels God to make an arbitrary choice:

> For to think that God acts in anything without having any reason for his willing, even if we overlook the fact that such action seems impossible, is an opinion which conforms little to God's glory. For example, let us suppose that God chooses between A and B, and that he takes A without any reason for preferring it to B. I say that this action on the part of God is at least not praiseworthy, for all praise ought to be founded upon reason which ex hypothesi is not present here. My opinion is that God does nothing for which he does not deserve to be glorified. (*Discourse on Metaphysics*)

Perhaps more difficult for Leibniz's optimism is the "problem of evil." Stated very simply—though it has cropped up in various different forms—this holds that the evil that exists in the world rules out the existence of an all-powerful, loving God. The problem then for Leibniz is this: His argument is that a perfect God will create a perfect world; the trouble is that it is obvious that the world is not perfect—just consider the effects of the Bubonic plague, for example; therefore, by his own lights, there cannot be a perfect God.

Leibniz was aware of this problem, and had a number of responses to it. For example, he argued that it is simply a mistake to suppose that it is possible to eradicate particular evils from the world and yet leave the rest of the world unchanged. Thus, for instance, while it might appear to us that the world would have been a better place without the Great Plague of 1665, we are actually in no position to make that judgment. He also questioned whether human happiness was necessarily the right measure for assessing the goodness of the world. As an alternative, he suggested that the best world is the one that is the "simplest in hypotheses and the richest in phenomena;" in other words, it is a parsimonious world.

Gottfried Leibniz

The Best of All Possible Worlds: Leibniz's philosophical position was satirized in Voltaire's Candide.

Monads

It is not only in the area of theodicy that Leibniz's philosophical optimism makes its presence felt; it also makes an appearance in his famous metaphysical theory of substances. It was Leibniz's view, certainly in the latter part of his life, that reality is constituted by infinite number of unities or monads. These are simple, nondivisible, soul-like entities, which lack extension, spatial position, shape, or indeed, any physical characteristics. Leibniz puts it like this:

> The Monad … is nothing but a simple substance, which enters into compounds. By "simple" is meant "without parts." And there must be simple substances, since there are compounds; for a compound is nothing but a collection or aggregate of simples … These Monads are the real atoms of nature and, in a word, the elements of things. (*The Monadology*)

On the basis of this initial conception, Leibniz is able to deduce a number of other characteristics of monads. For example, he argued that they only exist and can only be destroyed by divine intervention; that they have no "windows" through which anything can come in or out, so they cannot be affected by the actions of other entities, which means that they must be the sole source of their own activity; and that they are endowed with perception and appetition (the principle by which their perceptual states change).

What then of inanimate objects like tables, beds, and books? Surely Leibniz didn't think that these were built out of monads, which, after all, he thought were soul-like entities? The answer is that he did; but out of "bare monads," rather than the self-aware monads that are human minds. Liebniz's view was that monads are arranged in an infinite hierarchy; God, as the supreme monad, is at the top; human minds do pretty well, as a result of their capacity for rational thought and self-awareness; bare monads, only marginally percipient at all, come in at the bottom.

No doubt this all sounds very bizarre; not least because there is the question of how it is that it appears that things in the world interact with each other; given that Leibniz believed that monads are unable to affect each other, how is it that bodies, which comprise aggregates of monads, seem to do just that? It is here that Leibniz's philosophical optimism enters the picture. He argued that the regularities between monads were preestablished by a benevolent God; that monads were oriented toward each other in terms of a preexisting harmony. To put this another way, it was Leibniz's view that God had created the universe in such a way that the actions of any one monad will automatically be reflected in the actions of all others.

Leibniz's standing as a philosopher took a while to grow. Partly, as it has already been noted, he was damaged by Voltaire's satirical treatment of his philosophical optimism in *Candide*; and partly the fact that his work was not published in a systematic way meant that it took a while for people to appreciate its full significance. However, with the publication of *New Essays on Human Understanding*, his book-length criticism of Locke's *Essay*, written at the turn of the eighteenth century but not published until some fifty years after his death, his reputation began to grow. Today Leibniz is recognized as one of the greatest philosophers of the seventeenth century. Many of the concepts and ideas that are now a standard part of the philosophical armory—for example, the principle of sufficient reason, the identity of indiscernibles, and possible worlds— were introduced or foreshadowed in his work.

In common with a number of other philosophers, the last few years of Leibniz's life were not particularly good. In the aftermath of a row with the British scientific establishment over the originality of his differential calculus, he became embroiled in a bad-tempered correspondence with Samuel Clarke, a disciple of Newton, over the nature of space and time. Then, in 1714, his employer, Georg Ludwig, traveled to England to ascend the British throne as George I, but did not invite Leibniz to join him there, supposedly because he had not made sufficient progress with writing the history of the royal House of Brunswick. Two years later, on Sunday November 14, Leibniz died in Hanover at the age of seventy. He was buried a month later in an unmarked grave, which was hardly a fitting end for a man who had been celebrated in his lifetime as one of the seventeenth-century's greatest intellectual figures, and who would come to be recognized as one of the world's great philosophers.

MAJOR WORKS

Gottfried Leibniz only published one book in his lifetime, The Theodicy, preferring instead to set down his ideas in a series of short articles and voluminous correspondence. *The Cambridge Companion to Leibniz* is a good starting point to get a sense of this work; it also includes an essay by Roger Ariew, detailing Leibniz's life and works.

The Theodicy (1710)

Subtitled "Essays on the goodness of God," this work is primarily a defense of Leibniz's philosophical optimism as it relates to God. In particular, it contains a sophisticated response to the "problem of evil."

The Monadology (1714)

Not published until after his death, this is a short outline of Leibniz's view that reality is constituted by infinite number of unities or monads, and these monads are simple, nondivisible, soul-like entities, which lack extension, spatial position, shape, or indeed, any physical characteristics.

New Essays in Human Understanding (1765)

Written at the turn of the eighteenth century, but not published until some fifty years after Leibniz's death, this work is a detailed, critical discussion of and response to John Locke's *Essay Concerning Human Understanding*.

George Berkeley

George Berkeley (1685–1753) was the philosopher who made the radical claim that all that exists are minds and the ideas in them. Famously mocked by Dr Johnson, Berkeley's theory is more sophisticated than it may first appear.

1685–1753

There is a distinction between how things appear to us and how they really are. If you are in any doubt of it, put on a pair of shades. Either the act of putting on the shades resulted in the world quite literally darkening, or something else darkened, namely, your perception or inner representation of things in the world. Once this distinction is obvious to you, and you realize you are not directly aware of the material objects in the world but are aware of them in virtue of inner representations or mental images, it is possible to ask all sorts of worrying questions. How do we know that our inner representations match the way the world really is? All we have are the representations and no way to climb outside our skulls and compare them to the way things really are. Worse, how do we know that there is a world out there at all? This is the philosophical problem of the external world, and it is not an easy one.

Perhaps the most radical solution to this problem is that proposed by George Berkeley, and it consists in the outright denial of the existence of a material world underlying our inner experience. It is not difficult to be skeptical about the existence of external objects, if you take it that minds and the ideas in them are all that exists. This is precisely Berkeley's view.

If his philosophical position is radical, his life certainly was not, and there is not much in it to explain why Berkeley developed his extraordinary line of thought. He was born in Kilkenny, Ireland, attended Kilkenny College and Trinity College Dublin, eventually graduating and becoming a fellow himself in 1707. He was ordained into the Anglican Church three years later. It was during his years in Dublin that he formulated the arguments for his version of idealism, and he published the details in *The Principles of Human Knowledge* in the same year as his ordination. His position was almost instantly regarded as ridiculous, as proof of the madness of philosophers. Dr Samuel Johnson famously made sport of Berkeley by kicking a stone and proclaiming: "I refute him thus."

Quietly collecting himself, Berkeley tried again and published *Three Dialogues between Hylas and Philonous*, which patiently leads the reader through the motivation for the position and deals with objections to it. Though Berkeley's view is, to put it mildly, a little difficult to stomach, his writing is paradigmatically clear. The two books gained him a little ground—his easy and engaging personality gained him more—but he was welcomed into London intellectual life, perhaps as a kind of interesting curiosity. He traveled around continental Europe, became a fellow of

Trinity College, eventually Dean of Derry, and were it not for the publication of a slightly bizarre book later in his life, the remainder of Berkeley's time on Earth would suggest nothing of his unusual thinking.

His *Siris: a chain of philosophical reflections and enquiries concerning the virtues of tar-water, and divers other subjects connected together and arising from one another* was published in 1744. This deeply odd book contains more than a little mysticism coupled with a serious consideration of the benefits of drinking water mixed with pine resin. Berkeley's *Principles*, probably the most carefully argued and best articulated statement of idealism ever written, was largely ignored in his lifetime, as were his treatises on vision and motion. There were six editions of *Siris*.

Ideas and Minds

Berkeley's arguments for idealism begin with a distinction between ideas and minds. All the objects of human knowledge, Berkeley argues, are either ideas immediately experienced through sensation—such things as the taste of my coffee, the cool feel of the desk, the visual images I have on looking out of the window—or ideas we have on thinking about our emotional states, or ideas we form through acts of memory and imagination. We give names to sensory experiences that cluster regularly together. Round, smooth, red sensations of a certain sort we call "apples," and so on. In contrast to ideas, minds are active things: things that do the knowing, perceiving, sensing, willing, imagining, and remembering. A mind is not one of our many ideas, "but a thing entirely distinct from them, wherein they exist … whereby they are perceived; for the existence of an idea consists in being perceived."

This last point is worth emphasizing. Ideas can exist only in a mind. The taste of a lemon cannot exist outside of a mind, but only in the act of tasting or remembering a taste. The way my shirt feels, its texture and tightness around my wrists, can only exist so long as I am feeling it. Feels and smells need feelers and smellers, minds to occupy, otherwise they cannot exist. These seemingly simple observations are more or less all Berkeley needs to get his arguments under way, and we will have a look at several of them.

The claim that, say, tables and chairs can exist outside of a mind is self-contradictory, according to Berkeley. Tables and chairs are things we perceive by sensation; what we perceive by sensation are sensory ideas (this chair feels a little bumpy, looks grey and black, makes a kind of groan when I sit in it); "is it not plainly repugnant that any one of these, or any combination of them, should exist unperceived?" How could the feeling of bumpiness exist unfelt, outside a mind? The very idea of an unfelt feeling is self-contradictory.

Primary and Secondary Qualities

Stop right there, you might say. Plainly I have inner representations of things in the world, and some of the properties of these representations do depend on me, really are just in my mind. Something like the color of an object really isn't in the object; light bounces off of the object and affects me in a certain way, gives me the experience of seeing yellow, say. I know the object really isn't objectively yellow, yellow whether I look at it or not. Maybe the bumpy feeling is like this as well. But there

Berkeley radically—and controversially—claimed that "esse ist percipi"—that to be is to be perceived

are other properties an object really has, like its shape or position or whether or not it is moving, and none of this is mind-dependent. This is an appeal to Locke's distinction between primary (mind-independent) and secondary (mind-dependent) qualities, and Berkeley is having none of it.

Berkeley argues that the distinction collapses into nothing but mind-dependent qualities. One cannot imagine an object with primary qualities only. Berkeley maintains that "it is not in my power to frame an idea of a body extended and moving, but I must withal give it some color or other sensible quality, which is acknowledged to exist only in the mind."

If what is allegedly mind-independent is itself inconceivable without something mind-dependent, the allegedly mind-independent thing is mind-dependent after all.

You might try admitting that the direct or immediate objects of knowledge are inner representations, but go on to claim that representations really do represent something genuinely external, a mind-independent reality. Our visual images, for example, are representative copies of real things out there in the world. However, Berkeley argues that "an idea can be like nothing but another idea." To say that our ideas represent the world or parts of it is to claim that, for example, a color represents something out there which is itself never seen. Berkeley, almost audibly sighing, asks, "I appeal to anyone whether it be sense to assert a color is like something which is invisible."

What then accounts for the regularity of our perceptions on Berkeley's view? If so-called "physical objects" are ideas that exist only when perceived, what explains the fact that your sandwich is still there for you when you take it out of your rucksack? No one perceived it while it traveled to work with you, hidden away in your bag. Is Berkeley not committed to the absurd view that unperceived sandwiches wink out of existence when unperceived, only to reappear inexplicably at lunchtime? A materialist, someone who holds that matter really exists and underpins our sensory experience, has a quick answer to the reappearance of your sandwich: it actually existed all the while in the mind-independent world. Berkeley's world lacks a material substratum to underpin our perceptions. His solution to the problem is God.

MAJOR WORKS

Principles of Human Knowledge (1710)
Berkeley's masterpiece, and probably the clearest and best argued expression of metaphysical idealism in existence. In addition to arguments against materialism and abstraction, Berkeley makes plain the positive tenets of idealism, as well as a kind of proof of the existence of God.

Three Dialogues Between Hylas and Philonous (1713)
Guides the reader through the arguments for idealism in a dialogue form. It is a good thing to read after the *Principles*, as here Berkeley makes a deliberate effort to convince the skeptic.

De Motu or On Motion (1720)
A treatment of Newtonian physics in terms of Berkeley's own idealist views.

The Mind of God

If ideas, including your sandwich, can only exist when perceived, then some mind or other must have kept your sandwich in existence by continuing to perceive it when no one else could. Not just sandwiches, but the whole world continues when we take our eyes off it, and it continues not just in any way, but in a certain way. There are patterns and regularities for us to discover in the natural world. No finite mind is up to the job of keeping everything in the world in mind. Berkeley sees, in the very regularity of our perceptual experiences, a proof of God's existence, even his benevolence. Thus Berkeley: "… every thing we see, hear, feel, or in any wise perceive by sense, being a sign or effect of the Power of God."

This move clearly replaces one suspect thing with another. If Berkeley's arguments against a material substratum work by showing up inconsistencies or confusions or mysteries in the notion of substance, it will not do to substitute a divine mystery for a material one.

But Berkeley is happy with this sort of mystery. It is clear that at least a part of his motivation is a loathing of the cold, godless world afforded us by a certain conception of materialism. If the universe is nothing but matter in motion in space, there is not much room in it for morality and theism, and still less for the possibility that human life matters much in the grand scheme of things. In arguing for idealism, Berkeley saw himself as doing something about a dangerous line of thinking. He also thought his view was a remedy for skepticism about the external world, a restoration of the common man's beliefs. He maintains: "That the things I see with my eyes and touch with my hands exist, really exist, I make not the least question. The only thing whose existence we deny is that which *philosophers* call Matter or corporeal substance. And in doing of this there is no damage done to the rest of mankind, who, I dare say, will never miss it."

Whether or not Berkeley has produced a conception of the world consistent with the everyday man's outlook is an open question. Many, the mighty Hume included, read him as a kind of skeptic. However one characterizes his conclusions, it is clear, at least, that a reply to Berkeley must consist in something much more than merely kicking a stone.

Pulling rabbits from hats; the rabbit continues to exist when out of sight of the audience, according to Berkeley, because it is perceived by God.

David Hume

David Hume (1711–76) was the greatest Scottish philosopher, without question. Probably, he was the greatest philosopher of the eighteenth century, itself a century of greats.

1711–76

Hume might also be the greatest modern philosopher and the greatest empiricist; almost certainly he is the greatest philosopher in the skeptical tradition, a tradition perhaps closest to the heart of the impulse to philosophize. He is also the contemporary analytic philosopher's philosopher—promising graduate students are pointed to his work in the hope that something will rub off.

Hume was born in Edinburgh, his father's family a branch of the Earl of Home's and his mother's family a clutch of lawyers. Hume studied at the University of Edinburgh and was nudged toward the law, but he found an "insurmountable aversion" to everything but philosophy, literature, and history. He made up for his lack of funding by being frugal and industrious, and embarked upon a course of self-directed study. Whether or not this led to what some suspect was a nervous breakdown is unclear, but he quit his private researches and took employment as a clerk to a sugar merchant. Fortunately for us, he only lasted four months before being dismissed, and he then took up his studies again.

He moved to France in 1734 and wrote *A Treatise of Human Nature*; he came back to England with the hope of an excellent reception because of it. However, the book was almost entirely ignored. Hume laments: "It fell dead-born from the press without reaching such distinction as even to excite a murmur among the zealots." It was not, however, ignored by those who blocked his appointment to a professorship at the University of Edinburgh on charges of atheism and immorality. Hume never held an academic post.

There is a considerable difference between the perceptions of the mind and the later recall of those perceptions

Hume, as he himself puts it, "being naturally of a cheerful and sanguine temper … soon recovered" from his failure to attract interest with the book and published reworked portions of the *Treatise* in two slightly more digestible, smaller chunks entitled *An Enquiry Concerning Human Understanding* and *An Enquiry Concerning the Principles of Morals*. Again the British public were unmoved. (According to one commentator, it was likely that the only contemporaries able to understand Hume were Thomas Reid and Immanuel Kant. Both, arguably, spent their philosophical lives trying to deal with his conclusions.) Hume returned to France as assistant to England's ambassador, becoming a favorite in salon culture and something of a public figure. He published *The History of England* in 1754, and with it Hume at last achieved the fame he had sought; unlike his philosophical works, the book was read widely and ran to six editions. His *Dialogues Concerning Natural Religion*, published posthumously, easily joins the *Enquiries* and the *Treatise* as being among the most important philosophical books ever written.

The Study of Human Nature

Hume's aims in his philosophical writings are many, but perhaps the most important is his hope that something akin to the Newtonian reductive explanation of motion might be achieved with regard to the study of human nature. His aim is to "discover the secret springs and principles, by which the human mind is actuated in its operations." His discoveries are entirely skeptical: what we take to be warranted or justified beliefs in every domain that matters most to us are, in fact, founded on something other than reason.

Hume operates with many distinctions, and we need at least three in order to get his arguments going. The first distinction is between impressions and ideas: "There is a considerable difference between the perceptions of the mind, when a man feels the pain of excessive heat … and when he afterwards recalls to his memory this sensation or anticipates it in his imagination." The former are lively impressions and the latter are less forceful copies, or ideas.

The second distinction concerns the nature of ideas themselves: ideas might be either simple or complex. Following Locke, Hume argues that simple ideas cannot be broken down into still more simple ideas, while complex ideas are composed of two or more simple ones. It is important to note that simple ideas always have a corresponding simple impression in their first appearance, but this is not necessarily true for complex ideas. Thus, I get my simple idea of the taste of pineapple by tasting a pineapple, having the sensory impression. I might acquire a complex idea of a well-set table by looking at it. However, I might form my own complex idea, say, of a unicorn, by using my imagination to put together some simple ideas derived by impressions of horses and horns. I can be led astray into thinking my complex ideas correspond to something in the world, something experienced, when in fact they are mere fictions, products of the imagination.

The Five Ages of Man, from a baby to a skeleton. What, Hume asks, is it that endures throughout these changes?

Facts and Ideas

The third distinction is between "the objects of human reason or inquiry": relations of ideas and matters of fact. The former are propositions discoverable by the operation of thought alone, or armchair reflection. I can see the truths of mathematics and logic just by thinking about them, and in fact denying any such truth is self-contradictory. I can tell, for example, that $2 + 2 = 4$ is a relation of ideas because its negation or denial results in a contradiction. However, matters of fact depend on more than just thinking; I need to know how the world is in order to discover such truths. I need some experience to know that "It's raining outside" is true. Simply negating the proposition leads to no contradiction, does not help me one way or the other. Hume maintains that propositions are only of these two types, and only the relevant sort of evidence corresponding to each can justify our claims to know them.

These distinctions and a measure of ingenious reflection secure Hume the following three disturbing conclusions: reason has no hand in our beliefs in the self, the external world, or inductive inference. We will have a brief look at each.

On Causality

Suppose I claim to know that the president just resigned, and my evidence for this belief is a report in the newspaper I am holding. What I am doing, according to Hume, is going beyond the present evidence of my senses (the newspaper) by thinking causally—taking the newspaper report as the effect of a certain cause, the resignation. Causal thinking is, Hume argues, the only way we can move beyond the narrow band of present sensory experience, from the observed to the unobserved, from the present to the past and the future. Having had lots of experiences in the past of particular causes (political events) issuing in particular effects (newspaper reports), I expect that this cause-effect conjunction will continue to hold, and that the effect I see now is caused in the same reliable way as the past effects I have seen. What underpins our inference is the Principle of Induction: the future will be like the past. But, Hume asks, what justifies our belief in this principle?

The principle cannot be a relation of ideas, as its negation—the future will not be like the past—is perfectly conceivable, not self-contradictory. Nor can the principle be justified in terms of matters of fact, the truths discovered by experience, as this would be circular. We would be arguing that the future will be like the past, because in the past the future was like the past. This amounts to using induction to prove the principle of induction, and it is no justification. Instead of reason, Hume argues, custom or habit leads us to expect like causes to produce like effects. At bottom, nothing but human nature underpins our thinking in this connection.

What about our belief in an enduring self, the belief that we are persons or selves who persist over time? I think, when I see a photo of myself as a baby, that I'm looking at a picture of an earlier version of me. I also think, in a spirit of optimism, that I will still be that person for many more years to come. There must be something, the self, that endures through all the changes and makes me *me*. Hume admits that we have this idea, but to be a genuine idea it must come from some impression. Yet when he looks inward, introspects, he finds no unchanging impression to legitimize the idea. All he discovers is a constantly changing bundle of perceptions, but no enduring self. Hume concludes that the notion of a self is a fictitious product of the imagination.

Skepticism

Where do we arrive at the notion of objects that continue to exist distinct from our minds, the occupants of the external world, in other words? It is plainly impossible to arrive at this idea from sensation, as this would involve us in the absurdity of claiming that we have sensory impressions of objects that continue to exist when we do not sense them. Among other things, Hume points to Berkeley for a critique of the possibility that reason delivers the idea. If not sensation and reason, what else but the imagination could lead us to think that enduring objects exist?

It is not clear what to make of Hume's skeptical view of human rationality. Hume himself feels the tension, sometimes admitting that his conclusions have no force when he withdraws from his study and gets about the business of living. Elsewhere, though, what he thinks follows from his philosophy is clear enough. In this passage, Hume as librarian considers the worth of books about anything other than mathematics (abstract reasoning) or the reports of sensation (experimental reasoning). He writes:

> When we run over libraries, persuaded of these principles, what havoc must we make? If we take in our hand any volume; of divinity or school metaphysics, for instance, let us ask, *Does it contain any abstract reasoning concerning quantity or number?* No. *Does it contain any experimental reasoning concerning matter of fact and existence?* No. Commit it then to the flames: for it can contain nothing but sophistry and illusion.

We probably do not yet know the full implications of Hume's thinking because we are still catching up with him. What is depressing is that Hume might have left much more philosophy in the world had things been a little different. Had Hume been widely read and understood in his lifetime, he might have produced a great deal in response to criticism and questioning. It is hard not to regret philosophy's loss.

MAJOR WORKS

Treatise of Human Nature (1739)
Largely neglected in Hume's lifetime, but it is clearly one of the greatest and most important philosophy books ever written. Divided into three parts—on the understanding, the passions, and morals—it was intended as nothing less than a complete analysis of human nature.

An Enquiry Concerning Human Understanding (1748)
A shortened and more accessible version of book one of the *Treatise* and is probably the most interesting of Hume's shorter works. It contains his formulation of the problem of induction, speculation on causal necessity, a spectacular argument against belief in miracles, as well as instructive

thoughts on the nature of skepticism, along with much else.

An Enquiry Concerning the Principles of Morals (1751)
Hume's attempt to found a system of morality not on religious doctrine but on utility and sentiment.

Dialogues Concerning Natural Religion (1779)
Considered so controversial that it was published three years after Hume's death and did not include the publisher's name. It contains a series of brilliant objections to more or less all of the largest arguments for the existence of God.

Jean-Jacques Rousseau

Jean-Jacques Rousseau (1712–78) rose from humble beginnings to become a leading figure of the eighteenth-century French Enlightenment, alongside such giants as Diderot and Voltaire.

1712–78

Rousseau lived a life that was as colorful as the lives of any of the great philosophers. He was born in Geneva, the son of Isaac Rousseau, a watchmaker. His mother, Susannah Bernard, died very soon after his birth, and for the first ten years of his life he was raised by his father. It was during this time that he was introduced to the delights of literature. In his *Confessions*, he reported that he would sometimes spend all night with his father reading the romance novels that had been part of a collection of his mother's—an activity that resulted, he said, in an early interest in the passions. After 1719, he gravitated to more serious works, including Plutarch's *Lives* and Ovid's *Metamorphoses*.

These early years were very important for the development of his later political and social ideas. For example, his commitment to liberty and his sympathy for republican ideals had their roots in this period:

> Incessantly occupied with Rome and Athens, conversing, if I may so express myself, with their illustrious heroes; born the citizen of a republic, of a father whose ruling passion was the love of his country, I was fired with these examples; could fancy myself a Greek or Roman, and readily give into the character of the personage whose life I read; transported by the recital of any extraordinary instance of fortitude or intrepidity, animation flashed from my eyes, and gave my voice additional strength and energy. (*Confessions*)

In 1722, however, things changed for Rousseau; his father elected to leave Geneva as an alternative to imprisonment, after getting involved in a brawl; and Jean-Jacques was sent with his cousin to live in Bossey, a village not too far from their home town. He returned two years later to live with his uncle in Geneva, and then spent an unhappy and rather brutal period as an apprentice engraver. He eventually fled this situation, and on the advice of a Father de Pontverre sought out Madame de Warens, who had gained something of a reputation for securing Catholic converts, and entered her care. This was to be the making of him. Over the next ten years, he completed his education, discovered a passion for music, started to think in terms of a career as a man of letters, and in 1733, somewhat reluctantly, became Madame de Warens's lover.

This relationship did not last, and in 1742 Rousseau moved to Paris. If meeting de Warens had been the turning point of his youth, then this was the turning point of his adulthood. Quite soon after his arrival, having befriended the *encyclopédist* Diderot, he began to establish a reputation in Parisian intellectual circles. This exploded in 1750 on the publication of his first major work, *Discourse on the Sciences and Art*, which he wrote as an entry to a competition—which he subsequently won—and posed the question whether advancements in the sciences and arts had improved morals. In comparison with his later works, the thesis Rousseau advances in this essay is rather naive. However, it does set out what is perhaps the central contention of his life's work—namely, that the advent of civilization has in certain ways corrupted the natural goodness of human beings.

On Progress

His specific argument in this essay is that progress in the arts and sciences has always been accompanied by moral degeneration; sophistication in these realms is a function of idleness and a predilection for luxury, and it contributes to the decay of those societies where it is most marked. Thus, for example, as soon as Egypt, Athens, and Rome reached a certain level of cultural sophistication, decadence inevitably set in, and it wasn't long before they fell under the yoke of foreign powers. Rousseau recognizes that there will always be a few celebrated people able to make genuine contributions to humanity's fortunes; but as for the rest of us: "... let us remain in our obscurity. Let us not covet a reputation we should never attain, and which, in the present state of things, would never make up to us for the trouble it would have cost us, even if we were fully qualified to obtain it" (*Discourse on the Sciences and Art*).

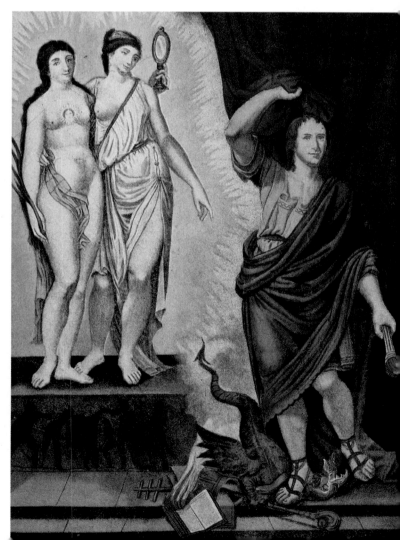

The Triumph of Reason and Truth; *philosophy, in the form of Jean-Jacques Rousseau, uncovers reason and truth, hidden from the universe by error and lies, in this late eighteenth-century engraving.*

The publication of this essay created a bit of a storm in French intellectual circles. It was perceived as a counterblast against the Enlightenment idea that the best hope for the betterment of humankind is the progress that occurs as societies throw off the vestiges of a past dominated by superstition and myth. Rousseau just didn't, in any straightforward sense, accept this idea, which became absolutely apparent with the publication of his second discourse on the origins of inequality.

In the first part of this he set out his idea of the "noble savage," or "savage man," who lives a solitary, peaceable existence concerned mainly with the fulfillment of immediate needs, and having little use for foresight, language, or any of the other things that come with a social existence. This idea stood in marked contrast with those of philosophers like Hobbes, who saw the life of man in a state of nature as nasty, brutish, and short. And, of course, that was the point; for it was Rousseau's intent to show that the vices of human beings exist because people live in social groups; and that as inequality inevitably emerges and then increases, so they are magnified.

Rousseau is not wholly clear about how "savage man" originally departed from a solitary life in a state of nature. He alludes to increases in population and the advantages of minimal cooperation in difficult times. However, what is certain is that once people began to enjoy fixed relations with each other, the conditions were ripe for the emergence of competitiveness, jealousy, and aggression:

> Everyone begins to survey the rest, and wishes to be surveyed himself; and public esteem acquires a value. He who sings or dances best; the handsomest, the strongest…the most eloquent, comes to be the most respected: this was the first step toward inequality, and at the same time toward vice. From these first preferences there proceeded on one side vanity and contempt, on the other envy and shame; and the fermentation raised by these new leavens at length produced combinations fatal to happiness and innocence. (*Discourse on the Origins and Foundations of Inequality*)

In Rousseau's view, even this situation would have been comparatively benign were it not for the emergence of private property. Indeed, Rousseau argues that civil society was effectively founded by the person who first enclosed and then claimed ownership over a piece of land; once there were people simple enough to believe the claim, civil society, as a means of justifying and maintaining property relations—that is, relations of inequality—was inevitable. At root, then, private property lies at the heart of inequality, and its associated moral turpitude.

The Social Contract

Rousseau did not think it was possible for humankind to return to a state of nature (indeed, he thought it likely that a state of nature never existed in precisely the form he specified). This, of course, leaves a problem: how are humans best to govern their affairs given present circumstances? It was this question that Rousseau sought to answer in his most famous work, *The Social Contract*.

MAJOR WORKS

Discourse on the Sciences and Art (1750)
The winning entry to an essay competition, it catapulted Rousseau to fame. Although clearly an immature work, its thesis that the advent of civilization has in certain ways corrupted the natural goodness of human beings proved highly contentious.

Discourse on the Origin of Inequality (1755)
An important critique of the ideas of philosophers such as Locke, this essay set down the idea that private property was the major source of the moral ills of modern societies.

The Social Contract (1762)
Generally, though not universally, considered to be Rousseau's masterpiece. It sets out the argument that sovereignty should express the general will of the social body, requiring that individuals when acting as members of that body set aside their own personal, sectional interests, and act only for the common good.

Emile (1762)
An essay on education, which argues for the possibility of a "natural" education, free of the corruptions of modern society, whereby people might be reared to be cooperative and respectful to their fellows.

The Confessions (1782)
Extraordinary autobiography, characterized by its honesty, which charts the course of Rousseau's life from childhood to old age.

In contradistinction to the concerns of Machiavelli, for example, in writing this work, Rousseau was primarily interested in the normative question of the legitimacy of sovereign power. The argument he constructed rests on the concept of "the general will." Prior to living in social groups, individuals are free to pursue their own specific, selfish interests. However, once people begin to live in fixed relations with other people, this kind of freedom is necessarily curtailed. Nevertheless, there is a way in which people may live in social groups yet remain free; that is, if each individual member of the group forms part of that group's sovereign body. Freedom then consists in acting in accordance with the "general will" of the group.

The "General Will"

The idea of the "general will" is more than a little slippery. It requires that individuals when acting as members of the sovereign body set aside their own personal, sectional interests and act only for the common good. Whether this is possible in practice is a moot point. Rousseau himself was clear that certain conditions would have to be met before it was even a possibility. Particularly, it requires the abolition of extreme wealth and poverty, and the existence of an educational system that would churn out citizens willing to act for the good of all. It also requires that the government, whatever form it takes (and Rousseau was not entirely prescriptive in this regard), separate and subordinate to the sovereign body, acts in line with the general will of the people.

Once people begin to live in fixed relations with other people, freedom is necessarily curtailed

Perhaps the major criticism that it is possible to level at the idea of the general will is that in effect it amounts to a dictatorship of the majority. This clearly was not Rousseau's intention; although he talked about people being "forced to be free," he was nevertheless committed to the ends of liberty and freedom. However, the problem is a real one, not least because it just isn't obvious that there is any such thing as a "common good"—it might just be that people have genuine but competing interests.

The Social Contract was published in 1762. This year marked something of a downturn in Rousseau's fortunes. Although he was at his intellectual peak, *Emile*, his treatise on education, attracted the attention of the authorities, and he was forced to flee Paris. Much of the writing of the remainder of his life constituted a defense of the positions he had set out in earlier work. He was also increasingly troubled by paranoia, becoming convinced that his old Enlightenment friends and sparring partners—Diderot, Voltaire, d'Alembert, and the others—were plotting against him, and he even suspected that David Hume, who had helped him travel to England, was part of the conspiracy. However, despite his difficulties, he was in the latter period of his life able to start and complete, among other works, his great autobiography, *Confessions*, which even by today's standards is remarkable in its candor.

He died in 1778 with his reputation assured. His commitment to liberty and equality meant that he was soon to become an important symbol of the French Revolution. His ideas even today retain their importance; not only are his major works part of the standard canon of political theory, he also remains an influential figure in thinking about communitarian and socialist politics.

Immanuel Kant

Ludwig Wittgenstein once remarked, and he may well have had Immanuel Kant (1724–1804) in mind, that reading philosophy is "a kind of agony." Kant's writing is spectacularly labyrinthine.

Kant's flair for inventing technical vocabulary is sometimes lost on those who notice the subtly different ways he uses those inventions, leaving the reader to keep track of the shifts with increasingly panic-stricken notes in the margins. His apparently morbid fear of punctuation results in sentences with lengths one never imagined possible—pages seem to float past as one loses all hope of a full stop. Despite all this, there is no question that Kant is among the very greatest of great philosophers.

Kant was born, lived, and died in Königsberg, Prussia (now Kaliningrad, Russia). Except for a few tentative, brief, and short-ranging excursions, he never left. He studied at the local high school, attended the University of Königsberg, and eventually took a post as lecturer there, becoming Professor of Logic and Metaphysics in 1770.

Kant's rigid habits were legendary. A well-known story has it that the housewives of Königsberg set their clocks by his afternoon walks, which he took with awe-inspiring regularity, his servant trudging dutifully behind with an umbrella in case of rain. His dinner parties were organized around a careful timetable, with precisely regimented portions of the evening spent in political discussion, the telling of amusing anecdotes, music, and so on. Guests reported that the evenings at Kant's were excellent affairs, with one accomplishing all one could hope to achieve in a single evening. Having become accustomed to the lifelong habit of breakfasting alone, he asked an unannounced friend to leave the table one morning, finding himself incapable of getting through the toast and tea in company.

It is not clear how much these stories should be believed, particularly as we do have the testimonies of many of his students, which do not quite agree with the stern caricatures above. The following is representative:

> In his prime he had the happy sprightliness of a youth; he continued to have it, I believe, even as a very old man. His broad forehead, built for thinking, was the seat of an imperturbable cheerfulness and joy. Speech, the richest in thought, flowed from his lips. Playfulness, wit, and humor were at his command. His lectures were the most entertaining talks.

Although Kant himself was not geographically wide-ranging, his lectures, early writings, and interests certainly were. He wrote and lectured on geography, mathematics, anthropology, physics, cosmology, and biology, as well as logic, metaphysics, and ethics. He continued his lectures, but did not publish anything for a period of nearly ten years. This was because Kant was quietly developing an entirely new approach to the fundamental questions of philosophy.

The Critiques

He broke the silence in 1781 with the publication of a masterpiece, *The Critique of Pure Reason*. Within a decade, this work was followed by two more of equal or nearly equal standing, *The Critique of Practical Reason* and *The Critique of Judgment*. And in the decade before his death in 1804, he published a number of other important books. The three Critiques contain nothing less than Kant's solutions to the main problems of metaphysics, ethics, and aesthetics. We will have a look at his ideas.

Kant notes that metaphysics has always seemed at war with itself. Arguments of apparently equal force might be leveled for and against the claims that the world has a beginning in time and is spatially limited, that every composite substance consists of simple substances, that free will exists, and that there is a God. Progress seems beyond us. We are compelled to wonder about these sorts of things, but when we bring reason to bear on them, we flounder in contradiction—or worse, despair in skepticism. Kant writes: "Human reason has this peculiar fate that in one species of its knowledge it is burdened by questions which, as prescribed by the very nature of reason itself, it is not able to ignore, but which, as transcending all its powers, it is also not able to answer."

This is particularly perplexing, as our rational capacities otherwise are essential to getting about the business of life. Kant proposes a critique or self-examination of reason, to determine its limits and proper employment. The hope is to end the otherwise interminable contradictions in metaphysics, as well as to provide some assurance that reason is a trustworthy guide when operating in its proper domain. Kant, then, calls upon:

> reason to undertake anew the most difficult of all its tasks, namely, that of self-knowledge, and to institute a tribunal that will assure to reason its lawful claims, and dismiss all groundless pretensions, not by despotic decrees, but in accordance with its own eternal and unalterable laws. This tribunal is no other than the *critique of pure reason*.

The Nature of Experience

Perhaps the best-known result of this critique is Kant's remarkable view on the role of the subject with respect to the nature of the experienced world. Before Kant, the mind was regarded as a passive recorder of the passing show. The metaphors for this view are familiar: the mind is the mirror of nature, like a blank slate upon which experience writes, like a lump of wax awaiting the impression of nature's signet ring. If the mind manages to conform to the way the world really is, the subject is said to know something about the world.

Kant turns this conception upside down. In what he described as a revolution of Copernican proportions, Kant maintains that the mind is active, playing a part in shaping the world of experience. Instead of

The question of free will remains an open one in Kant's philosophy.

knowledge consisting in our minds conforming to a world of objects, Kant maintains that objects must conform to our minds.

This is much more than a mere reworking of Locke's claim that some properties are mind-dependent—that such things as color and smell are not in the objects themselves, but depend upon a relation of subject and object. Rather, Kant holds that the mind categorizes and organizes all that is received in sensory experience in the forms of space and time and further shapes this input with such categories as cause and substance. The mind plays a part in the nature of the whole empirical world.

How does this revolution solve the problems of metaphysics? Since objects must conform to the powers of the mind in order to appear to us as objects in the first place, our knowledge of objects is knowledge of appearances. The very notion of an appearance presupposes something more, namely, a reality beyond appearances. Kant makes a distinction, then, between appearances (phenomena) and things-in-themselves (noumena), things as they are apart from experience. We can know something about appearances, but we can only think about things-in-themselves, and this is why metaphysics leads to contradictions. Metaphysical inquiry is an attempt to know things-in-themselves in terms of categories proper only to the world as we experience it.

Because causation is the result of our mind's categorizing activities, reason rightly looks for causes when events are perceived—a world of objects in space and time is unthinkable without causation. However, when we attempt to apply the concept to the universe as a whole, as it is in itself, and wonder whether or not the universe itself is caused, we have wandered beyond reason's proper domain, and contradictions are unavoidable.

This line of thinking shows why all speculative metaphysics is suspect, but it makes knowledge of the empirical world possible, and assures reason a secure role in our understanding of the phenomenal world. While Kant undercuts metaphysics, he nevertheless leaves room for certain truths. Think again about causation. If it is not possible to think of the world as we experience it without the concept of causality, then for the empirical world, every event has a cause. There is no appearance of human freedom. This view leaves open the question of whether or not human beings, considered as things-in-themselves, really are free. With the question of free will open, there is room for morality.

Doing the Right Thing

Kant's conception of morality is firmly rooted in reason, and it is a departure from other accounts which claim that morality must be based on sentiment or even the consequences of action. For Kant, doing the right thing is not a matter of one's character or disposition or circumstance—all of which are or might be beyond one's control. Instead, it is a matter of duty, acting out of respect for the moral law. The moral law, Kant argues, cannot be hypothetical in nature, cannot be of the form, "If you want such and such, do so and so." Wants and consequences cannot figure into what is morally right. Instead, the law itself must be categorical, of the form, "Do this" or "Don't do that." Kant offers the following formulation of the so-called "categorical imperative": "Act only on that maxim whereby you can at the same time will that it should become a universal law."

An example, Kant's own, might make all of this more clear. Suppose the rent is due, and you are in serious financial difficulty; your troubles are likely to be unending for the foreseeable future. You approach a friend for a loan, and she agrees, with the proviso that you promise to repay it by next week. You know this is impossible, but you contemplate making the false promise anyway, knowing there is no chance of repaying the loan.

Kant argues that actions are undertaken under maxims or rules, and the rule you are contemplating is this: "When I think I need some money, I will borrow it and promise to repay it, though I know I never can do so." Kant's test for such maxims is universalizability: suppose the maxim you are considering were to become a universal law, a maxim adopted by everybody. Would the system thus engendered be consistent or self-contradictory? If the former, you are in no danger of doing the wrong thing, but if the latter, you are in violation of the moral law. If everybody made false promises, promising itself would be impossible—who would believe a promise? The maxim you were contemplating results in a self-contradiction, and it is therefore not in keeping with the categorical imperative. Don't do it.

The morality pie can be cut in lots of ways, but a large slice is reserved for the Kantians, and arguments between duty-based ethicists and consequentialists show no sign of slowing down. It is probably not possible to understand much in contemporary ethics without knowing at least the bare outlines of Kant's thinking. It is certainly impossible to understand German philosophy since Kant without knowing a great deal about Kant himself. His view of the human mind as somehow actively constituting the empirical world, radical in his day, is now an obvious presupposition in many quarters.

Although Kant himself did not travel, it is clear that his thinking is now everywhere in philosophy.

MAJOR WORKS

Critique of Pure Reason (1781)
Kant's masterpiece and one of the most unusual and philosophically impressive books ever written. Its most astonishing insight is the claim that the mind plays an active role in constituting the objects of knowledge.

Critique of Practical Reason (1788)
Contains Kant's formulation of the moral law and an in-depth discussion of the relation between the ideas of God, human freedom, immortality, and the very notion of morality.

Critique of Judgment (1790)
Kant's consideration of aesthetics, in particular the judgments we make about the nature of the beautiful and the sublime.

Thomas Paine

Thomas Paine (1737–1809) would play a part in bringing about the American revolution with his political essays and pamphlets; however, his later work would lose him friends in America.

1737–1809

Thomas Paine was born in Thetford, England, on January 29, 1737. For the next thirty-seven years, he lived a life of impressive mediocrity. He failed in a variety of professions, including teaching, tobacco selling, and tax collection. His marriage was something of a disaster, with some biographers reporting that even before formally separating from his wife in 1774, Paine had never lived together with her. And when, aged seventeen, he had attempted to run away to sea, he was captured on board ship by his father, who carried him back home again.

Paine's early lack of success was not entirely surprising. Unlike many of the great philosophers, he had not been born into privilege. His father Joseph Paine, a Quaker, was a corsetmaker by profession. This did not bring in much money. Indeed, Thomas Paine recounted later that it had cost his parents some hardship to send him to the local grammar school: "My parents were not able to give me a shilling, beyond what they gave me in education; and to do this they distressed themselves."

However, though Paine's early years were inauspicious, there were aspects of his upbringing that left an indelible stamp on his character, and which informed the political writings that were later to make him famous. In particular, the Quakerism of his father gave him the strong sense that all human beings are born fundamentally equal and the moral courage required to pursue a reforming agenda.

One of the strongest natural proofs of the folly of hereditary right in kings, is, that nature disapproves it.

The transformation in his fortunes, when it came, happened very quickly. In October 1774, on the recommendation of Benjamin Franklin, whom he had met when seeking to interest parliament in a tax relief measure, he had sailed for America. He carried a letter of introduction written by Franklin, and on the strength of it he was able to secure a job, first as a writer for *Pennsylvania Magazine*, and then as its editor. It was here that he wrote his first notable article; a call for the abolition of slavery, which he signed off "Justice and Humanity."

Common Sense

He followed this up with the essay that was to make him famous. "Common Sense" was published early in 1776, and it had an immediate impact. In it, Paine argued that it was both a moral duty and practical necessity for America to seek independence from Great

Satirical cartoon by Gillray, depicting Thomas Paine's Nightly Pest, *an unpleasant vision of what would await him should he ever return to Britain.*

Britain. He attacked the idea of a hereditary monarchy, partly on the grounds that it violated a principle of equality that is rooted in the natural condition of humankind:

> For all men being originally equal, no one by birth could have a right to set up his own family in perpetual preference to all others for ever, and though himself might deserve some decent degree of honor of his contemporaries, yet his descendants might be far too unworthy to inherit them. One of the strongest natural proofs of the folly of hereditary right in kings, is, that nature disapproves it, otherwise she would not so frequently turn it into ridicule by giving mankind an ass for a lion.

For Paine, it was unthinkable that America should continue to be ruled by a British king. He argued that such an eventuality would result in North America being kept as low as possible by their master. He also claimed that American independence, and the establishment of a republican form of government, founded on the principle of the equality of its citizens, was the best way of avoiding the possibility of civil conflict.

There is no doubting the influence of "Common Sense." It not only persuaded many of the major figures in the American Revolution of the merits of an independent America, but it also sold in large numbers—120,000 in the first three months after publication—to the general populace. Paine continued his writing to great effect throughout the War of Independence. Indeed, shortly before the battle of Trenton, George Washington had called his demoralized soldiers together in groups so that Paine could be read aloud to them in order to improve their morale:

> These are the times that try men's souls. The summer soldier and the sunshine patriot will, in this crisis, shrink from the service of his country; but he that stands it now, deserves the love and thanks of man and woman. Tyranny, like hell, is not easily conquered; yet we have this consolation with us, that the harder the conflict the more glorious the triumph: what we obtain too cheap we esteem too lightly; it is dearness only that gives everything its value.

The Rights of Man

After the war, Paine briefly held a couple of government jobs, before returning to England where he wrote what is perhaps his most important work, *The Rights of Man*. It was a primarily a defense of the principles of the French Revolution against the criticisms that Edmund Burke had leveled against it in his *Reflections*. Developing a theme which had first appeared in "Common Sense," Paine argued that people are born with equal, natural rights. However, they do not live as isolated individuals, but rather in societies where they enjoy the benefits of cooperation and sociality. Unfortunately, in such circumstances, it is almost inevitable that from time to time the rights of people will be violated, because human beings are far from perfect. Consequently, in order to secure all natural rights, people will deposit those rights which they cannot uphold individually—for example, the right to redress for a harm—into the protection of government.

According to Paine, this means that government is only legitimate when it is established by the people as a whole; that is, government must be of the people, and for the people. This rules out hereditary monarchy straight away, because this form of government involves a previous generation determining the rulers of future generations. In fact, it was Paine's contention that the only legitimate form of government is democratic republicanism; it best represents the aggregate rights that people are unable to defend individually, and which they therefore give up to government in order that all rights are secured.

Perhaps more radically, Paine also used *The Rights of Man* to outline in some detail a system of welfare, with the aim of addressing the social deprivation associated with poverty. He noted that the gallows seemed to be the exclusive province of the poor, and argued that this was a sign of government gone wrong:

> Why is it, that scarcely any are executed but the poor? The fact is a proof, among other things, of a wretchedness in their condition. Bred up without morals, and cast upon the world without a prospect, they are the exposed sacrifice of vice and legal barbarity. The millions that are superfluously wasted upon governments, are more than sufficient to reform those evils, and to benefit the condition of every man in a nation, not included within the purlieus of a court.

All this proved too much for the British establishment. In May 1792, a royal proclamation was issued against seditious writing, and Paine was charged with treason, causing him to flee to France, never to return. At first, he was welcomed in France, even gaining a seat at the National Convention. However, things soon became difficult for Paine. He was denounced by the Jacobin leader Robespierre for his association with the Girondins, a moderate republican group, and was arrested very soon after completing his book *The Age of Reason*, in which he argued for deism against both atheism and Christianity.

Paine very nearly lost his life in the Jacobin Terror, but was eventually freed when the American statesman James Monroe intervened on his behalf. After his release from prison, Paine carried on writing. In *Agrarian Justice*, published in 1797, he returned to questions of social justice and basic rights. He argued that the mark of a civilized state *ought* to be that it leaves no individual worse off than they would have been had they been born before civilization existed. However, he noted that in fact the poor in every country in Europe were worse off than the native American Indians of North America. He put this down to the fact that more than half the inhabitants of every nation had been dispossessed of landed property.

The proper response to this situation is not collective ownership, as was suggested by Karl Marx more than 100 years later, but rather a system of land and property tax, with the proceeds going into a National Fund and then being redistributed among all the people of a nation. Paine emphasized that this was not a matter of charity, but of rights. As inhabitants of Earth, every person has an equal claim over Earth in its natural state. The proposed National Fund would compensate for the fact that most people—for sensible reasons—were unable to succeed in this claim.

Reason and Superstition

In 1802, Paine returned to America, the land where he had first made his name. However, he was much less popular on his return than he had been when he had left some twenty years earlier. His arguments in *The Age of Reason*, particularly his attacks on the vengeful and spiteful God of the Bible, had alienated many in the New World. Consequently, though he continued writing until his death, Paine lived out the remaining years of his life in ill-health and obscurity.

There is a parallel here with how Paine has been treated by history. Although his writings were hugely influential during his lifetime, and he has remained something of a hero to people on the British Left, he is not normally considered to be in the top rank of philosophers. This is partly because his work lacks the sophistication and learning of people like John Locke and Karl Marx. However, to criticize Paine for this reason would be to misunderstand the intent of his writing. He was addressing a popular audience. He had the ability—which all too many philosophers lack—to write in a clear prose style; of affecting people, and getting them to see their traditional attitudes and values in a new light. To read Paine even today is still to be struck by the power and integrity of his voice.

MAJOR WORKS

"Common Sense" (1776)
The essay that made Thomas Paine famous. Exploding on to the scene in the middle of the War of Independence, it argues for the independence of America from Great Britain, both on moral and practical grounds.

The Rights of Man (1792)
A defense of the principles of the French revolution against the criticisms set out in Edmund Burke's *Reflections on the French Revolution*. Its central thesis is that the only legitimate form of government—of the people, and for the people—was democratic republicanism.

The Age of Reason (1794)
This work outlines the case for an enlightened deism, but perhaps more significantly includes an assault on the vengeful God of the Christian Bible, which alienated many of Paine's supporters in the New World.

Agrarian Justice (1797)
This book argues for a system of land and property tax, with the proceeds going into a National Fund, and then being redistributed among all the people of a nation. Paine emphasizes that this was not a matter of charity, but of rights.

Georg Hegel

Georg Hegel (1770–1831) occupies a rather strange position in the history of philosophical thought: he is both extremely influential and almost impossible for a nonspecialist to understand.

1770–1831

Hegel's dialectical method is best understood in terms of the concepts of thesis, antithesis, and synthesis

Two of Hegel's most important works, *The Phenomenology of Spirit* and *The Science of Logic*, contain some of the most difficult philosophical writing that has yet appeared. Indeed, the impenetrability of his prose has led some people to suspect that he was a charlatan; that he deliberately obfuscated in order to create the appearance of profundity where, in fact, none existed.

However, this is to be uncharitable; Hegel's is a systematic philosophy—indeed, he is arguably the last great system builder in philosophy—and at least some of the difficulty of his work is linked to the magnitude of the task he set himself. His aim was nothing less than to develop the conceptual apparatus necessary to understand the whole of reality, or, as he called it, Absolute Spirit. But even so, close reading of his work will eventually bear fruit; certainly it is possible for readers without a background in philosophy to get something from texts like *Lectures on the History of Philosophy* and *The Philosophy of Right*.

Hegel was born in Stuttgart on August 27, 1770. As the son of an official in the government of the Duke of Württemberg, he enjoyed a comfortable, middle-class upbringing. He was educated at the local grammar school, and although he did not show the precocious abilities of Blaise Pascal or the American philosopher Charles Sanders Peirce, he was nevertheless a first-class student. His taste for systematic and methodical work was evident even in these early years; as a schoolboy, he kept a diary in which he carefully charted the progress of his reading; and at the age of sixteen, he started an alphabetized collection of the detailed notes he took from the books he read.

His father wanted him to become a clergyman, so in 1788, Hegel entered the Protestant seminary at Tübingen. Although he successfully completed his studies there, his teachers reported that while he had excelled in philosophy, he had not appeared particularly interested in theology. Not surprisingly, then, he decided against a career in the Church, and instead pursued his ambition to attain an academic position; this he achieved, with the help of his friend Schelling, when he took up a post at the University of Jena in 1801.

It was while he was at Jena that Hegel put together *The Phenomenology of Spirit*, probably his most famous work. In it, he attempted to show, roughly speaking, how consciousness develops via a dialectical process, until it recognizes that it is identical with the whole of reality, which itself is pure thought or spirit. Unfortunately, this idea is every bit as complex as it sounds. Perhaps the most fruitful way to gain a sense of it is to consider what is involved in the idea of dialectical progress.

The Dialectical Method

Hegel's dialectical method is best understood in terms of the concepts of thesis, antithesis, and synthesis. Put simply, the idea is that any given phenomenon (thesis) contains within itself contradictory aspects (antithesis) that require a movement toward resolution (synthesis); and that progress in our understanding of reality occurs according to an iterative process that has this dialectical form. It is possible to illustrate this idea by looking at how Hegel thought that an individual self-consciousness moves toward self-certainty.

The idea of self-certainty is a complex one; however, it seems to be most clearly expressed by the notion of "belongingness." Hegel had in mind that self-consciousness aims toward a situation where there is nothing in external reality that is alien to it; where, in a strong sense, self-consciousness is synonymous with the reality that it constitutes. Part of the significance of this journey to self-certainty is that it underpins the original relationship between self-consciousness and things that are other to it.

In Hegel's scheme, self-consciousness emerges when consciousness recognizes the reflection of itself in the objects toward which it is directed. Thus, "consciousness of another, of an object in general, is in fact necessarily self-consciousness, reflectedness in self, consciousness of oneself in one's other." However, while self-consciousness requires an external object to define itself, it is at the same time threatened by this object. The external object is foreign to the self; it is an otherness, in the face of which self-consciousness is unable to attain self-certainty. Thus, in a state of *desire*, self-consciousness seeks to negate the otherness of the external object by assimilating it. In the words of Hegel, "self-consciousness presents itself here as the process in which this opposition is removed, and oneness or identity with itself established."

However, with the negation of the otherness of the external object comes a difficulty: if this entails the object's destruction, then self-consciousness, dependent upon the moment of otherness, is robbed of the foundations of its own existence.

Therefore, self-consciousness requires an object that can be

Title page of Hegel's Philosophy of History. *This is one of the most accessible of Hegel's works, despite its 480-page length.*

negated, whose foreignness can be annulled, without the object itself being destroyed. According to Hegel, only another self-consciousness fulfills this requirement, since only this is able to effect its own negation, and yet remain an external object. Specifically, he claims that a self-consciousness must seek the acknowledgment and recognition of other self-conscious beings; only in this way can it attain the self-certainty it desires.

Master and Slave

With this insight, therefore, that "self-consciousness exists in itself and for itself, in that, and by the fact that it exists for another self-consciousness," we are led to the famous dialectic of master and slave. Although mutual recognition between self-consciousnesses will ultimately bring the self-certainty that these seek, this will not be easily won. At first, neither self-consciousness is certain of the truth of the other—as self-consciousness —and hence both are deprived of the source of their own certainty. Consequently, each will try to attain the recognition of the other without reciprocating.

According to Hegel, the resulting struggle—for one-sided recognition—is necessarily to the death, because, in risking their own lives, these self-consciousnesses can demonstrate to each other, and to themselves, their freedom from their particular bodily forms, and hence their status as *beings for themselves*. However, it is clear that in this context the death of either participant would be irrelevant, since it would completely deprive the survivor of recognition. Hence, the solution to the struggle for one-sided recognition, which must put the life of each participant in danger, is the enslavement of one and the mastery of the other: "The one is independent, and its essential nature is to be for itself; the other is dependent, and its essence is life or existence for another. The former is the Master, or Lord, the latter the Bondsman" (*The Phenomenology of Spirit*).

However, it is Hegel's view that the opposition between individuals is something that will in time be overcome. The dialectic of master and slave, and the conflict that this entails, is simply one of the phases

MAJOR WORKS

Phenomenology of Spirit (1807)

Hegel's most celebrated work. Employing his characteristic dialectical methodology, it tracks the unfolding of Being, or Absolute Spirit, across the whole of history. It is an extraordinarily difficult book, but also hugely influential, setting in motion a whole tradition of philosophy in the nineteenth century.

The Science of Logic (1812–1816)

It sets down, systematically and in detail, the basis of Hegel's metaphysical logic. The dialectical method is employed in order to articulate the abstract categories of thought, with the conclusion in the end being that reality is constituted by the Absolute.

Elements of the Philosophy of Right (1821)

The most mature statement of Hegel's social and political philosophy. In it, Hegel suggested that the most rational state was similar to the existing Prussian monarchy. For this he was accused of selling out, and it led the Young Hegelians to develop their own version of Hegelianism, one which in their eyes was nearer to the spirit of the real Hegel.

Lectures on the Philosophy of History (1833–1836)

One of the easiest entries into Hegel's ideas, compiled from lecture notes after his death, it tracks the progress of freedom across time and in the context of different kinds of society.

that self-consciousness must pass through on its way to self-certainty. Interestingly, it is the slave, and not the master, who takes the next steps on the journey; transformed by the experience of work, the slave comes to possess the intellectual tools necessary to progress to a greater self-understanding.

The Philosophy of History

Hegel employed a similar dialectical method in order to analyze the unfolding of human history. In his view, human history is characterized by the move toward greater freedom, rationality, and understanding. As he put it in the introduction to *Lectures on the Philosophy of History*, "The history of the world is none other than the progress of the consciousness of freedom."

In this book, which was compiled from lecture notes after his death, he tracked this progress of freedom through the examples of various kinds of society. Thus, in ancient oriental regimes, such as China, only the despot is free; the people who make up the populace of these societies lack even the knowledge that they have the ability to make autonomous judgments. Although Hegel thought that the citizens of the city-states of ancient Greece enjoyed a certain truncated freedom, he said that it was only with the Reformation that the idea of individual freedom found proper expression. History from this point on can be understood as the series of changes that societies underwent in order to get to grips with this new concept of freedom. Thus, the Enlightenment, though it led to the excesses of Jacobin terror, and demonstrated that there could be no absolute break with the past, was nevertheless an attempt to reconstruct modern societies in terms of the precepts of abstract universalism.

In Hegel's view, once an awareness of freedom has come to exist, it will eventually triumph; and, in an echo of Rousseau, he said that politics then is about building communities that enable individuals to live out a freedom based upon their common ability to reason.

Hegel's ideas have had enormous impact on social and political thought over the last two hundred years. Most famously, Marx employed Hegel's dialectical method in the development of his historical materialism; indeed, in the early part of his life, Marx, along with people like Bruno Bauer and Ludwig Feuerbach, considered himself to be a young Hegelian. Sartre's existentialism was also heavily indebted to Hegel; particularly, his analysis of being-for-others is predicated on a development of the insights contained in the master and slave section of *The Phenomenology of Spirit*.

However, it is also true that the kind of philosophy that Hegel represents—namely, the tradition that is fond of grand metaphysical speculation—has fallen on hard times. In particular, the rise of logical positivism in the twentieth century, with its claim that statements are meaningful only if they are true by definition or empirically verifiable, undermined the appeal of a philosophy like Hegel's. A. J. Ayer, for example, in his *Language, Truth and Logic*, had no difficulty in showing that Francis Bradley's Hegelian inspired version of idealism was constructed out of claims that were not in any obvious way meaningful. Indeed, for many people working in the analytic tradition of philosophy, Hegel's kind of philosophy is precisely what has to be avoided in order to produce good work. Therefore, whatever one thinks about the merits of his philosophical system, it is almost certain that we won't see the like of Hegel again for quite some time.

John Stuart Mill

John Stuart Mill's (1806–73) father, James Mill, was an outspoken advocate of utilitarianism and a friend of Jeremy Bentham, its founder. John Mill was born into a household steeped in utilitarian thinking, particularly Bentham's views on education.

1806–73

It was the aim of Mill's father to educate the boy himself, in his own words, to turn him into "a mere calculating machine." This James Mill more or less did, with alarming consequences.

John Mill could read Greek at the age of three and Latin at eight. According to his autobiography, by his early teens he had read all the major Greek and Latin works, made an extensive survey of history, and become well versed in jurisprudence, psychology, economics, mathematics, and logic. His father lectured to him on such subjects during long walks, requiring him to write up the lectures for consideration the next day. James Mill based a book, *Elements of Political Economy*, on a set of these papers. John Mill was just fourteen at the time.

At fifteen, Mill read *Theory of Legislation*, the first published account of Bentham's utilitarian views. The book changed him comprehensively: "I felt taken up to an eminence from which I could survey a vast mental domain, and see stretching out into the distance intellectual results beyond all computation." It gave Mill a standpoint, a philosophical position rich enough to underpin views across the philosophical spectrum, and, he hoped, the means to improve human life generally. His whole life really had prepared him for just this revelation. "When I laid down the last volume of the [*Theory*]," he says with some reverence, "I had become a different being." In addition to pursuing the study of law, the new Mill spent the remainder of his teens editing many of Bentham's unpublished manuscripts, contributing to several journals with papers on current events, political debates, and law, all from the utilitarian point of view.

At twenty, perhaps predictably, the calculating machine suffered the worst of a series of nervous breakdowns, or at least deep bouts of depression. Already in a "dull state of nerves," Mill reflected critically on his own happiness. He asked himself if he actually would be happy if all his aims were realized, if all his planned improvements to institutions and law were effected. On discovering that not even this could please him, he plummeted into a kind of hopeless anguish. Mill had been well-prepared for argumentation and analysis, but it seems he had no training to help him cope with the vagaries of emotion. It will send a Freudian chill down your spine to learn that he was brought out of this depression while reading about a boy who became an inspiration to his family following the death of his father. It perked Mill up, and he returned to his work, supplementing it with a new interest in poetry, culture, and the arts—which, it seems, formed a part of the cure too.

Utilitarianism

Mill became probably the foremost English-speaking thinker in the nineteenth century, and certainly he is among the most influential and wide-ranging. In addition to studies of jurisprudence, economics, and psychology, his philosophical work spans analyses of language, logic, and mathematicss, as well as scientific methodology. He has clear views on the relationship between inner mental states and the external world, formulating the first expression of phenomenalism, the view that physical objects are permanent possibilities of perception. It is, however, his writings on ethics and politics that have received the most attention, most notably *Utilitarianism* and *On Liberty*.

Mill seems to be saying the life of a dissatisfied intellectual is to be preferred to an idiot's life of simple pleasures

Mill's general aim in *Utilitarianism* is to defend and expand upon Bentham's view that good acts are those that produce the greatest happiness for the greatest number of people. Happiness is construed here, as it is in Bentham's writings, in terms of the intrinsic worth of pleasure. Although the book is a complicated one, we'll consider just one aspect of Mill's defense and one aspect of Mill's expansion on Bentham's conception of utilitarianism.

Suppose we think along the following lines, like a good utilitarian. Acts that produce the greatest happiness for the greatest number are good. It is the end, happiness, that makes actions good. Happiness itself is understood in terms of pleasure, and it is pleasure that has a special sort of value for the utilitarian. What proof have we that pleasure has this sort of value, the sort of value that carries a moral consequence, namely, that we ought to pursue it as an end? In one of the most perplexing passages in the book, Mill seems to offer the following proof:

> The sole evidence it is possible to produce that anything is desirable, is that people do actually desire it. If the end which the utilitarian doctrine proposes to itself were not, in theory and in practice, acknowledged to be an end, nothing could ever convince any person that it was so.

The claim seems to be that pleasure is actually desired by everyone, so it is, therefore, desirable, valuable in the required way for a moral demand, something we ought to pursue. Mill goes on to say that the only things visible are things seen; the only things audible are things heard. Similarly, the only things desirable are things desired, and what everyone desires is pleasure. First of all, it is not clear that the analogy works. Visible things are things that can be seen; audible things are things that can be heard. Mill needs it to be true that things desired are things that *ought* to be desired, not things that *can* be desired. As Russell puts it, the argument is "so fallacious that it is hard to understand how he can have thought it valid."

After all, Mill is proposing a moral system: everyone ought to act in such a way that actions bring about a greater balance of pleasure over pain. The proof of the claim that people ought to desire pleasure

MAJOR WORKS

System of Logic (1843)
An expression of Mill's radical empiricism. In it he argues that even the laws of logic are empirical in nature. The work also includes an important consideration of induction.

On Liberty (1859)
Deals with the conflict between minority rights and the rule of a democratic government. It contains the excellent suggestion that an individual ought not be compelled by a government to do something merely for his own good.

Utilitarianism (1861)
Mill's attempt to expand upon Bentham's conception of utilitarianism. In particular, Mill offers a treatment of the qualitative aspects of pleasure and pain.

cannot be just that people do desire pleasure. We cannot infer what ought to be the case from what actually is the case. Further, what becomes of the moral weight of utilitarianism if it turns out that Mill is right? What is the point of arguing that people ought to desire pleasure if they are going to desire pleasure anyway?

Second, is it true that people in fact desire pleasure? For Mill's line of argument to work, it has to be true that when I desire something, I desire that thing because of the pleasure getting it will give me. My desire, really, is for pleasure. This may sometimes be so, but when I desire candy, for example, I really do desire candy first and foremost—the pleasure is, for me, a secondary thing.

You can complicate the question, if you like, by thinking about the possibility of individuals who explicitly deny that they desire pleasure. A masochist might tell you that they desire pain, maybe muddying the waters by explaining that they derive pleasure in a secondary way from their ultimate desire, pain.

Mill's expansion on Bentham's conception of utilitarianism consists in part in a consideration of not just the quantity of pleasure derived from an action, but its quality. Bentham's hedonistic calculus, complex as it was, does provide an algorithm for choosing between actions on the basis of the amount of pleasure produced, but it does not take account of distinctions between the quality of different pleasures. Mill takes it that some pleasures are of a finer quality than others, and further that such higher pleasures are more desirable than others. Why think the so-called "higher pleasures" are more valuable than the base ones? Further, is there a clear way to tell the difference between them? Mill's answers might be gleaned from this passage:

> Few human creatures would consent to be changed into any of the lower animals, for the promise of the fullest allowance of a beast's pleasures; no intelligent human being would consent to be a fool, no instructed person would be an ignoramus, no person of feeling and conscience would be selfish and base, even though they should be persuaded that the fool, the dunce, or the rascal is better satisfied with his lot than they are with theirs.

Mill's claim here is that a person who has experienced both back rubs and poetry, both a full stomach and Mozart, will notice something having to do with the purity, sublimity, depth, and refinement of higher pleasures which leaves base pleasures far behind, no matter the quantity. A person who has experienced both sorts of pleasure will be able to tell the difference between them and see that one is of a different and preferable kind to the other.

You will recall that Mill cured his depression, in part, with the finer things in life, and it might be that this clouds his judgment. He seems to be saying that the painful life of a dissatisfied intellectual is to be preferred to an idiot's life of simple pleasures. Is this compatible, at all, with the principle of utility?

Much of what Mill claims in *On Liberty* clearly follows from reflections on utilitarian principles coupled with Mill's view of what is best in us, our capacity for self-improvement and the determination of our own routes to happiness. Mill maintains that self-development, individuals pursuing their own aims, is among "the essentials of human well-being." Thus, individual liberty gets star billing in Mill's politics. He argues for the following curb on the powers of government: "… the only purpose for which power can rightfully be exercised over any member of a civilized community, against his will, is to prevent harm to others. His own good, either physical or moral, is not a sufficient warrant."

It is possible to wonder just how far Mill departs from Bentham in this connection. Bentham's initial aim in working out the principle of utility was to provide lawmakers with a way of coming to reasoned conclusions about what is best for everyone. A Benthamite lawmaker ought to formulate laws for the good of the citizens, ought to curb individual activities in an effort to make the citizenry happier. Mill denies this explicitly. People should be able to do what they like, even to the extent of jeopardizing their own happiness, so long as they harm no one else.

This is not as far from the letter of utilitarianism as one might think. Mill maintained that the state that adopts this principle has happier people in it than one that does not. Given the alarmingly comprehensive powers of modern states over their citizenry, and the regular attempt on the part of such states to justify their more dubious activities in terms of what is best for us, it is hard not to think Mill was right to want to restrict political power in this way.

It is illegal to ride a motorcycle without a helmet. However, to compel an individual to do something simply for their own good, says Mill in On Liberty, *is an abuse of democracy. Many would maintain that the same holds true for compelling people to refrain from—potentially—harmful actions.*

Søren Kierkegaard

Søren Kierkegaard (1813–55) is generally recognized as the first existentialist philosopher. Unlike many other existentialists, there is a strong theological vein running through his philosophy.

1813-55

Kierkegaard's life was in many respects unremarkable—for example, he only ever left his native Denmark on three occasions, and his leisure time was spent mainly visiting the theater and walking in Copenhagen—yet it is not possible to appreciate his work properly without knowing something about his biography. Fortunately for us, Kierkegaard kept voluminous journals from the age of twenty-one, which help with the task of understanding how his life and philosophy connect together.

He was born on May 5, 1813 in Copenhagen, and was the youngest child of Michael Kierkegaard, an affluent Danish businessman, and Ane Sørensdatter Lund, the one-time maid of his father's first wife. His father, the most significant figure of his youth, was a deeply religious man who was committed to a particularly pietistic form of Lutheranism, and was racked with chronic feelings of anxiety and guilt. Some commentators locate the source of these feelings in an incident from his childhood where he had cursed God from the top of a hill after becoming exhausted and cold while tending sheep, while others point to the possibility that he impregnated his second wife before he married her. Whatever the truth of the matter, he passed on his pessimistic and gloomy religious outlook to his son, who later described his upbringing as "insane" and wrote in a journal entry that he had come into the world as the result of a "crime."

The sense of foreboding that permeated Kierkegaard's early years was compounded by the premature deaths of his mother and five of his brothers and sisters. It was his father's belief that this was a sign of divine retribution; indeed, he did not expect any of his children to survive beyond the age of thirty-four, and with the exceptions of Søren and Peter, his eldest son, he was proved right.

Given this background, Kierkegaard's education was surprisingly normal; he attended a celebrated private school—Borgedydskolen—where he was lonely, aloof, and intellectually the superior of his classmates; and then, at the age of seventeen, he went to the University of Copenhagen with the aim of studying theology. This didn't quite go to plan. There followed a brief period of what passed for teenage rebellion in nineteenth-century Denmark. At university, Kierkegaard became more interested in philosophy and literature than theology; and he adopted the lifestyle of a party animal, drinking, smoking, and running up debts, which his father then had to settle.

Ethics and Aesthetics

However, in 1838 his father died, and this seems to have brought an end to Kierkegaard's career as a bon vivant. He turned his attention back to his theological studies, and two years later gained his master's degree. It was also at this time that he became involved with Regine Olsen in the only real love affair of his life. As is well documented in his journals, he proposed to her, immediately regretted it, spent a year equivocating, and eventually broke off the engagement in 1841. The reasons for his behavior are not entirely clear; however, it would appear that he came to the view that his melancholic temperament was unsuited to marriage; that he was intellectually incompatible with her; and that his vocation as a writer meant that he could not commit himself to marriage.

Without a doubt, the affair profoundly affected him. It crops up time and again in his journals, and also appears, thinly disguised, in his philosophical works. For example, he uses parts of *Either/Or*, one of his first major publications, to work through the various issues that motivated his decision to break with Regine. Similarly, another early work, *Repetition*, tells the story of a young man unable to marry the woman he loves because he fears the ethical commitment that marriage requires. Of course, there is more to these works than merely the effort to exorcize a few psychological demons; they also have serious philosophical points to make.

In *Either/Or*, he sets out two modes of existence by which people might live their lives. The first, the aesthetic mode, which is articulated in the papers and letters of a person called "A," is hedonistic in character, emphasizing the importance of immediate gratification and living in the moment. The ethical mode, in contrast, is built on duty and obligation. It is conveyed in two letters to "A" that analyze and criticize his motives and prospects, and suggest that in order to achieve fulfillment he should commit himself to the kinds of continuous projects that would constitute an ethical life. Kierkegaard's own view about the right choice here was disguised by his use of unusual narrative techniques and multiple pseudonyms. However, he quickly came to the view that

MAJOR WORKS

Either/Or (1843)
Sets out a view of two modes of life, the "aesthetic" and the "ethical." The aesthetic is hedonistic in character, emphasizing the importance of immediate gratification and living in the moment. The ethical mode, in contrast, is built on duty and obligation. Kierkegaard came to the view that neither mode of life was satisfactory.

Repetition (1843)
This work tells the story of a young man unable to marry the woman he loves, since he fears the ethical commitment that marriage requires. Clearly, influenced by Kierkegaard's doomed affair with Regine Olson.

Fear and Trembling (1843)
An analysis of the conflict between the demands of ethics and religion, strikingly illustrated by the story of Abraham, required by God to kill his son. Kierkegaard argues that to obey this instruction requires behavior that is completely outside the domain of normal morals; it necessitates a suspension of the ethical in the service of a higher *telos* (goal).

The Concept of Anxiety (1844)
Focusing on the pervasiveness of anxiety in the stage of life that precedes religious faith, this work makes the claim that anxiety is linked to an awareness of human freedom, the inevitability of sin, and the requirement of radical choice.

neither the aesthetic nor the ethical mode were adequate; rather there existed a third mode of existence, the religious sphere, where humans might find true freedom and fulfillment.

The Leap of Faith

The religious sphere is constituted by a "leap of faith," made in "fear and trembling," which takes it outside the domain of rationality. The Christian's worship of the God-man Jesus, who is both temporal and eternal, is necessarily paradoxical. It is simply not possible to appeal to rational argument or empirical evidence to justify such a belief; all that is available is passionate commitment. In his book *Fear and Trembling*, Kierkegaard spells out what this might mean for ethics by looking at the biblical story of Abraham and Isaac.

In Genesis, the first book of the Bible, God commands Abraham to kill his son Isaac. According to Kierkegaard, obeying this instruction requires behavior that is completely outside the domain of normal morals; it necessitates a suspension of the ethical in the service of a higher *telos* (goal). He illustrates this by comparing the situation of Abraham to that of a "tragic hero." To take a modern example, consider the following scenario: A military commander knows that if she wants to prevent the destruction of a city, then she must send a battalion of her soldiers to their certain deaths; the battalion includes among its number her son. This constitutes a very difficult moral dilemma, but it lends itself to rational discussion; whatever course of action the commander chooses, she will be able to offer a justification for it that other people will understand. This is not the case with Abraham. He must simply follow a command, which comes to him from above, that will have a consequence that is absolutely unthinkable in terms of normal moral discourse. Not only can he not justify his actions to other people, he cannot even tell himself a story to explain why it is required of him. All that counts is his passionate commitment to a subjective, felt relationship with God.

Proper religious faith can only be achieved with great difficulty

Religious faith then is not an easy option, and indeed, according to Kierkegaard, proper religious faith can only be achieved with great difficulty. So why choose it? Why not remain wedded to the aesthetic and ethical modes of existence? The answer is that it is only by religious faith that individuals can avoid despair and find their true selves in the freedom that, paradoxically, dependence upon a transcendent being brings.

In emphasizing the irrational and subjective dimensions of the religious mode of existence, Kierkegaard is also making a wider point about the futility of attempts to achieve objective knowledge of the totality of human thought and experience by the means of a rational, logical, systematic, metaphysical framework. His particular target here is Hegelianism, which, in the middle part of the nineteenth century, was the dominant philosophical approach in Denmark. In its totalizing imperative, Hegelianism is necessarily flawed; for example, with respect to religion, it aims to make God and the Christian faith transparent to reason, whereas in fact they remain necessarily outside the domain of rational understanding.

This also ties in with the unusual way in which Kierkegaard presents his arguments. Nearly all of his important philosophical works were published pseudonymously; they also make heavy use of irony, satire, and humor to make their points. This was in the service of a method

Kierkegaard called "indirect communication." The idea was to deprive his readers of the comforts of authorial authority, thereby compelling them to make their own judgments about where they stood on particular issues and arguments. Kierkegaard drew a link here with the way that Socrates encouraged his interlocutors to think for themselves by undermining their standard responses to the questions he asked. This method is driven by his ongoing commitment to the importance of individual choice and responsibility.

Kierkegaard always recognized that his work would not find favor while he was alive; indeed, he predicted that it would only be in the twentieth century that the significance of his writings would be appreciated. He was largely right. The first book written about him was not published until 1877, twenty-two years after his death at the age of forty-two; and although he became well known in Germany in the early part of the twentieth century, it wasn't really until the period between the two world wars that he came to be considered a major intellectual figure. Obviously, the emergence of existentialism had a lot to do with this, because the themes that Kierkegaard examined in his work are similar to those that were explored by philosophers like Heidegger and Sartre. Particularly, his emphasis on the importance of individual freedom, and the responsibilities and burdens that it brings, is a thread that runs through nearly all existentialist thought.

Of course, not everybody has good things to say about Kierkegaard. There is, for example, the suspicion that the core of irrationality that lies at the heart of his philosophy is all too easily transfigured into a kind of nihilism, or even fascism. After all, as Voltaire made only too clear, many terrible things have been justified on the basis of appeals to faith (and, indeed, Kierkegaard himself had some pretty reactionary social views). Nevertheless, his importance as a philosopher is without question; by insisting that individuals and subjectivity, freedom and passion, are important, Kierkegaard helped to bring philosophy down from the clouds, where it had been in danger of floating off on a Hegelian wind.

Abraham prepares willingly to sacrifice his son Isaac, in obedience to God's command. According to Kierkegaard, religious observance such as this lies outside the realm of everyday morals, necessitating a suspension of ethical judgment.

Karl Marx

By some measures, Karl Marx (1818–83) is the most important of the modern philosophers, in the sense that it is impossible to understand the history of the twentieth century without reference to his ideas.

1818–83

The revolutions in Russia and China were both, at least ostensibly, Marxist in character. The Second World War turned out in favor of the Allies partly because Hitler, blinded by his hatred of communism, ordered an invasion of the Soviet Union. And the Cold War pitched Western-style capitalism against societies that identified themselves as socialist or communist.

Marx's influence, of course, is not a matter of pure happenstance. He wrote with the intention of changing the world. Thus, his *Communist Manifesto*, written with his friend Friedrich Engels, ends with a call to arms:

> The Communists disdain to conceal their views and aims. They openly declare that their ends can be attained only by the forcible overthrow of all existing social conditions. Let the ruling classes tremble at a communist revolution. The proletarians have nothing to lose but their chains. They have a world to win. Workers of all countries, unite!

There was little in Marx's early life to suggest that he would become modernity's exemplary political radical. He was born on May 5, 1818 in the Prussian city of Trier on the banks of the Mosel. His father, Heinrich Marx, was an interesting fellow. A successful lawyer, he converted from Judaism to Christianity shortly before Karl was born, largely to protect his business from Prussian anti-Semitism. Heinrich was a disciple of the Enlightenment, and he introduced Karl to the writings of great Enlightenment thinkers, such as Leibniz, Voltaire and Kant, and also to liberal political ideas.

The young Marx was a forceful personality. His sisters later recounted how he bullied them relentlessly, but made up for it by reading them stories. He shone at school in literary subjects—though he wasn't so good at mathematics and history—and it was the intention that he should follow in his father's footsteps and become a lawyer, so, in 1835, he went off to the University of Bonn to study law. But a year later, he moved to the University of Berlin, switched from law to philosophy, and hooked up with a group of radical thinkers, members of the Young Hegelian *Doktorklub*. It was at this point that Marx's radicalism came to the fore. He identified himself as left-wing, committed himself to democratic politics, and espoused atheism.

Unfortunately for Marx, his newly found radicalism put paid to any hopes of finding an academic job. In 1842, having successfully completed his doctorate, he began the first of a number of jobs editing radical journals. The next few years were probably the most important in the development of his thought. Crucially, in 1844 he began a lifelong friendship with Friedrich Engels (1820–95), the son of a textile manufacturer. It was Engels who introduced Marx to the emergent working-class movement, and also to the study of political economy. This point marks the emergence of a recognizably Marxist social and political philosophy.

It is sensible to strike a cautionary note here. Marx was not straightforwardly a philosopher. It would perhaps be more accurate to describe him as a social or political theorist. His inclusion in a book of this sort is warranted, first, because his work is steeped in philosophy; and second, because he has influenced many philosophers, particularly those working in continental Europe. However, the fact that his work covers a broad range of subject areas—philosophy, economics, political theory, and history, among others—makes it hard to summarize. Or rather, it means that any summary will be necessarily selective. But having said that, it is certainly possible to identify some of the key themes in Marx's thought.

Marx and Human Nature

Perhaps the best jumping off point if we want to understand Marxist theory is to consider how Marx viewed human beings. In other words, did he have a theory of human nature? The answer to this question is an equivocal yes. Marx did not think of human nature in the same terms as, say, a contemporary sociobiologist; he was not, for example, interested in the specification of particular human instincts. But he did think that it was in the nature of human beings to cooperate in a process of collective, freely chosen labor. His idea was that humans come to full self-realization in the process of transforming the world in their own image through their labor. This is quite a complicated notion—which is not surprising, given that it has an antecedent in the philosophy of Georg Hegel—but perhaps a sense of it can be attained by imagining a team of engineers who put body and soul into producing a fantastic building; when they subsequently gaze at the building, it isn't too fanciful to think that they see something of their own humanity, of their productive sociality, in their creation.

Marx did think that it was in the nature of humans to cooperate in a process of collective, freely chosen labor

The importance of this idea that human beings come to full self-realization through freely chosen labor is that it underpins the concept of alienation, which in turn is the lynchpin of Marx's criticism of societies that are characterized by class conflict. Put simply, people are alienated when they are separated from the products of their labor and from the labor process itself. This occurs when they lose control over the circumstances in which they engage in productive activity and over the products of their labor. The key point about alienation is that it is always self-alienation. For Marx, to be alienated is to be separated from one's essential humanity; it is to be unable to live a fully human life.

Self and Alienation

Alienation, in varying degrees, is a facet of all class societies; that is, all societies where there is a division between those people who own and control the means of production and those who do not. However, it is in capitalist societies that alienation reaches its zenith. Capitalism is characterized by a fundamental conflict between two great, antagonistic classes, the bourgeoisie, the owners of the means of production (i.e. factories, machinery, etc.), and the proletariat, who own only their own labor power. The proletariat are alienated because they are forced to sell their labor under circumstances not of their own choosing. They have little or no control over the labor process, and their productive energies are expended for the benefit of the class that exploits them. Marx describes the proletarian's experience of alienation thus:

> …he does not fulfill himself in his work but denies himself, has a feeling of misery rather than well-being, does not develop freely his mental and physical energies but is physically exhausted and mentally debased. The worker, therefore, feels himself at home only during his leisure time, whereas at work he feels homeless. His work is not voluntary but imposed, forced labor. It is not the satisfaction of a need, but only a means for satisfying other needs.

However, all is not lost for the proletariat, for it was Marx's view that they are the bearers of the emancipatory potential of humankind. Capitalism is not indestructible; indeed, according to Marx, it is riddled with contradictions, which in the end will result in its downfall; and it is the proletariat who will bring this about. Specifically, as a *class-for-itself*, a class aware of its own reality and situation, it is the destiny of the proletariat to abolish all class distinctions, instituting a new form of society—communism—based on collective ownership; in doing so, they will end the alienation of people from the products of their labor, from the labor process itself, and from their essential humanity.

At this point, the Marxist account runs into difficulties; capitalism is still going strong, and the proletariat, if they exist, do not seem to be aware that they are supposed to be a revolutionary force. So what's gone wrong? Was Marx just incorrect about all this?

It is possible to be charitable here. Marx was aware that capitalism had resources at its disposal to allow it to counter the effects of its internal contradictions. For example, you'll find that Marxists make a big play about something they call "false class consciousness." The idea here is that the working class are not aware of their historic destiny as a revolutionary force because they have been exposed to capitalist ideology. The bourgeoisie, as a result of

The House of Trade Unions in Moscow, with multilingual proclamations and banners of "fathers" of the Marxist state, Marx, Engels, Lenin, and Stalin during the Stalin era.

their domination of the economic sphere, also control things like the educational system and the mass media. Therefore, they are able to get their ideas out into society at large, with the result that the proletariat remain blind to their true situation. In Marxist parlance, the proletariat never make the transition from a *class-in-itself* to a *class-for-itself*.

It is, of course, also possible to argue that capitalism has not crumbled yet, but that it will; that Marx might have been wrong about timescales, but that he got the fundamentals right. This kind of argument is often coupled with an analysis of the way in which capitalist economies have managed to exploit new markets, for example, in the developing world. However, there is something philosophically suspect about this move; the claim that something has not happened yet, but that it is sure to happen at some point in the future is unfalsifiable and there is more than a whiff of blind faith about it.

Moreover, it isn't clear that Marxism is rescued even if one grants that capitalism might one day come to an end. The problem is that the Marxist idea that capitalism will be replaced by a society free of systematic inequality and conflict just isn't very plausible. Perhaps wisely, Marx didn't have a lot to say about the precise form that communism would take. He suggested that people in communist society—rational, self-aware, and other-directed—would no longer be estranged from each other or themselves. His friend Engels envisaged a day when state power and the government of people would not be necessary.

The question is whether, from the perspective of the twenty-first century, this is a plausible vision of the future. Probably it isn't. But having said that, it is perhaps slightly unfair to hold Marx up to the standards of twenty-first century knowledge when accusing him of flawed understanding. Not least, he had not experienced the horrors of the twentieth century when putting his theories together. It is not implausible to think that with the kind of hindsight that the last century leaves us with, Marx might have been less optimistic about human potential and the possibilities for a world without fundamental conflict.

MAJOR WORKS

Paris Manuscripts (1844)
A series of extracts on philosophy and economics, primarily notable for the first proper expression of Marx's ideas on alienation.

German Ideology (1846)
Co-written with Friedrich Engels, and published only posthumously, the doctrine of historical materialism was first expounded in this work.

The Communist Manifesto (1848)
Classic and polemical statement of Marx's revolutionary philosophy of history, it became the manifesto of many a communist party. It pursues the political implications of the fact that "the history of all hitherto existing societies is the history of class struggle."

A Contribution to the Critique of Political Economy (1859)
Noted for its Preface, which is a succinct expression of the materialist philosophy of history.

Capital (3 Volumes: 1867, 1884, 1893)
Marx's definitive and most famous work, still uncompleted at his death. Primarily a work of political economy, it constitutes an exhaustive account of the workings, and failings, of capitalist society. The second and third volumes were edited and published by Friedrich Engels.

William James

William James (1842–1910) was the brother of the novelist Henry James. Along with C.S Peirce, James would achieve his own recognition with the founding of the first homegrown American school of philosophy, pragmatism.

1842–1910

In 1905, William James (1842–1910) recorded the following entries in his diary, as he considered the possibility of retiring from professional teaching: October 26th, "Resign!"; 28th, "Resign!!!"; November 4th, "Resign?"; 7th, "Resign!"; 8th, "Don't resign"; 9th, "Resign!"; 16th, "Don't resign!"; 23rd, "Resign"; December 7th, "Don't resign"; 9th, "Teach here next year." He continued at Harvard until somehow managing to resign in 1907. You can form the impression from this, probably rightly, that James's mind moved in several directions at once. Possibly this trait nearly killed him, but the resolution he came to became pragmatism, the first home-grown American philosophical movement.

Many commentators trace James's breathtaking indecisiveness to the fact that he spent his childhood in a kind of benevolent upheaval. James's grandfather, an Irish immigrant, was a multi-millionaire, and, following his death, James's father Henry enjoyed financial independence. This was probably just as well, as Henry James was something of a restless intellectual, with religious aspirations but no head for business, and the income enabled him to pursue his interests and devote himself to his children's education. The five children—James's brother Henry was the well-known novelist—were taught to think freely and fiercely, with breakfast table topics ranging as widely as their interests carried them. The family moved regularly back and forth between the United States and Europe, largely with the aim of gaining the best possible education for the children. They spoke many languages between them and had a decidedly cosmopolitan tolerance for the beliefs of others. James was able to see virtually every side of every argument or possible choice, the merits and disadvantages of all.

While this is usually an attractive character trait, it led to James's near-paralysis with respect to life choices. James suffered from insomnia, bad eyesight, and back problems all his life, but there was also always an undercurrent of depression compounding the physical misery. Some argue that his depression grew from his inability to come to the conclusion that what he was doing with his life was right in the face of the many alternatives his disposition easily brought into view. His family moved to Rhode Island so that James could study art—some of his excellent portraits survive and are worth a look—but he dropped

Believe that life is worth living and your belief will help create the fact

it within a year and enrolled in the Lawrence Scientific School at Harvard. Still unsure that the laboratory bench was the right place for him, he took a place at the Harvard Medical School. He interrupted this with a year-long expedition to the Amazon with the bizarre anthropologist Louis Agassiz. He found himself nearly middle-aged and with no clear idea of what to do with his life.

On Determinism

This uncomfortable feeling was made worse by philosophical worries about the possible truth of determinism. What difference could a life make if every action, thought, and hope were caused by prior events? What meaning could a life have at all? At the heart of his crisis, too, was a conflict between religion and science. James's father came under the influence of the dubious Emanuel Swedenborg, and spent a life working through his own conception of religious belief. No doubt James felt some pressure to adopt his father's religiosity. However, James himself, though possessed of no small artistic and literary talent, felt drawn to the hard facts of scientific inquiry. The pain of this conflict, as well as his directionless life, combined with the possibility that there was no free choice available that might lead to a resolution, was nearly too much for him. Suicide became a serious consideration.

A philosophical conversion seemed to save him. James read the work of the French philosopher Charles-Bernard Renouvier and found in it an unusual solution to the problems posed by determinism. Renouvier argues that free will consists in "the sustaining of a thought because I choose to when I might have other thoughts." One might not be able to choose which thoughts come into the mind, but an act of will can focus the mind on some thoughts at the expense of others, thoughts that then determine action. It led James to the view that neither the thesis of determinism nor free will is provable, leaving room for a kind of choice based on the practical consequences of adopting one or the other position. James opted for free will and, in so doing, seemed to get it. Here is a kind of kernel of pragmatism, as we shall see.

James got himself under way. He was commissioned to write a textbook on the new science of psychology. Predictably, it was published ten years behind schedule and did not resemble a textbook in the slightest. It was *The Principles of Psychology*, and its influence was

Empathy on the battlefield. James argued that no matter how hard one tries, it is impossible to fully empathize with another's pain.

immediate, lasting, and large.

The book is positivist in flavor, and attempts to make the psychological study of mind a part of natural science, showing how mental life and visible bodily life are connected. The mark of the mental, for example, becomes a question of identifying the characteristic behavior of things with minds. According to James, such things exhibit plastic or flexible goal-directed behavior—they make choices that enable them to get what they want despite obstacles. James, under the sober influence of Darwin, is then led to reasonable reflection on the point and purpose of mind from an evolutionary point of view. Put a minded thing up against a mere automaton, and the minded thing will outperform the mechanism every time.

Perhaps the most interesting part of the book is the chapter on consciousness, which James famously characterizes as "the stream of thought." Breaking with the traditional view of, say, sense perception as repeatable inner images—seeing the same dead ant on your nightstand today as yesterday involves the same thing happening in conscious experience—James argues that consciousness is in a constant state of flux. Consciousness, for James, is also personal: it is owned or belongs to someone, with all the mental baggage this entails. As such, the vagaries of personal circumstance do more than just flavor experience, ensuring that the stream is always changing; circumstances make the various streams distinct. No matter what your powers of empathy are, you will never feel my pain.

James's consideration of the self broke with tradition too. Instead of talk of ghostly souls or some other substance on which to hang the draperies of personal identity—what it is that makes you you over time—he distinguishes between the "I" and the "me." The material me is made up of objects to which I have a kind of emotional attachment or personal interest: family, friends, and valued possessions. The social part of me consists in the roles I play in different social circumstances. Cherished values make up the spiritual me. My best hopes for me are the ideal me. The "I" for James is closer to the usual notion of ego or self, but he identifies it with something nearly Aristotelian: a kind of activity that consists in one's present thinking.

Pragmatism

Following the publication of *The Principles of Psychology*, James seems to have all but dropped his interest in psychology for philosophy, attempting in particular to reconcile the tension he felt between the religious impulse and the hard-headed demands of scientific inquiry. The result is an articulation of pragmatism, a term borrowed from his friend Peirce, who argued that pragmatic concerns should guide our understanding of truth and meaning. James fleshed out the view in accord with his own concerns. His expressed contention that philosophy ought to be concerned with the lives of everyday people is responsible for another large difference between James and Peirce. James's writing is much less technical than Peirce's. With James we get a little less clarity in exchange for a lot more readability.

James's opinion of pragmatism certainly had something to do with his escape from suicide. Truth, for James, consists partly in the usefulness of an idea, and usefulness is a complex matter. The simple-minded objection to pragmatism, that it is nothing other than a free license to believe whatever makes a person feel a little better, misses at least a part of the point. Usefulness for James depends not just on the extent to which an idea pushes one toward a better life, but also on the predictive power an idea might confer—the view is in line with James's radical empiricism. James also argues that an idea of x is only a useful idea if it helps one deal with x should x exist. Truth really does correspond to reality for the pragmatist. Further, ideas must be consistent with other ideas to stand a chance of being true. There are elements of coherentism here too.

The emphasis, though, is clearly on what difference the idea makes for practical affairs. As James puts it:

> Pragmatism asks its usual question. "Grant an idea or belief to be true," it says, "what concrete difference will its being true make in anyone's actual life? How will the truth be realized? What experiences will be different from those which would obtain if the belief were false? What, in short, is the truth's cash value in experiential terms?"

The view provides a decision procedure for dealing with metaphysical disputes. To use James's example, suppose you were circling a tree, trying to have a glimpse of a squirrel that is matching your movements around the tree too. If someone asks, "Are you going around the squirrel?" you can interpret the question in at least two ways, but what possible difference to human conduct could your answer make? Philosophical disputes are often merely linguistic in just this way. Where there's no difference for practice—no cash value—there's no difference at all.

James is subject to considerable criticism concerning his religious views. He argues that empirical evidence cannot decide the matter of God's existence, and so a part of the decision consists in plumping for the belief that most improves life. Belief in God wins, just, because it leads one to a better attitude toward the future and puts some much-needed meaning into a life.

Can one really just will to believe something like this? Apparently, James both thought so and did so. You can hear something of the escape from suicide in all of this. It certainly was James's view that philosophy should take some of the sting out of existence, as it clearly did for him. He urges us to "[b]elieve that life is worth living and your belief will help create the fact." One can quibble with James's arguments, but it is hard to find a reason to object to his motivations.

MAJOR WORKS

The Principles of Psychology (1890)
James's long and bold treatment of mind. It includes his famous account of the stream of consciousness, the "I" as opposed to the "me," and free will.

The Will to Believe and Other Essays in Popular Philosophy (1897)
A collection of papers on such topics as rationality, determinism, morality, and the meaning of life. It expounds James's view that some questions force a choice even when the evidence is inconclusive. On such occasions, some answers contribute to a better life than others, and this gives us a right to believe them.

The Varieties of Religious Experience (1902)
James's study of human nature, in particular that aspect of human nature which is concerned with religious experience.

Pragmatism (1907)
A collection of lectures on the pragmatic theory of truth, meaning, knowledge, and the pragmatic method of resolving philosophical questions.

Friedrich Nietzsche

Friedrich Nietzsche (1844–1900) remains one of the nineteenth century's most misunderstood and misquoted philosophers. His most notorious concept, however, that of the Superman, is in fact closer to Aristotle's man of virtue than it is to some glorified Aryan hero.

1844–1900

Friedrich Nietzsche was influential, controversial, disturbing, systematically misunderstood, and very good fun to read. It is his excellent prose that initially attracts many of us. You can easily spend an afternoon gorging on his words, by turns smiling at his wit and gasping at his dark pronouncements. You can then spend a lifetime working out his meaning.

Nietzsche's short life began on October 15—the birthday, too, of his namesake Friedrich Wilhelm IV, the King of Prussia—in Röcken, Prussia. His father, Ludwig, was a Lutheran minister and his mother, Franziska, was the daughter of a Lutheran minister. What bearing this surfeit of Lutheranism had on his scathing treatment of religion is worth thinking about. So too is the fact that Nietzsche's father lost his mind when Nietzsche was only five—there is some speculation about the unlikely possibility that Nietzsche's insanity was inherited. Following his father's collapse, he, his sister, and his mother lived with the maternal side of the family: two aunts and a grandmother. Nietzsche obtained an excellent classical education in a famous boarding school and eventually took a place at the University of Bonn to study theology. He quickly abandoned theology for philology at the University of Leipzig, toying momentarily with the possibility of studying chemistry. It was at Leipzig that Nietzsche discovered his three great early influences: Schopenhauer, the materialist F.A. Lange, and Wagner. It was also at Leipzig that Nietzsche probably contracted syphilis.

Following a brief stint in the military, cut short due to a chest injury caused by the pommel of his saddle while he was mounting his horse with excessive exuberance, Nietzsche rather astonishingly was offered the Chair in Philology at the University of Basel. He had not completed a doctoral thesis, but the enthusiasm of his tutors and Nietzsche's great gifts carried him through to the post. He was just twenty-four.

He soon took leave to serve as a medic in the Franco-Prussian war, and on his return to the university was plagued by dysentery and diphtheria. Although he got to work on his first book and undertook the usual teaching duties, Nietzsche was never well. He had suffered from a number of health problems since early childhood—migraines, insomnia, poor eyesight, and stomach upsets, which were probably the result of ulcers. His old illnesses coupled with his new ones finally forced him to retire from the post. He spent the remainder of his sane life shambling between boarding houses in constant ill-health—he once confided that the possibility of suicide was his only comfort—writing and publishing a remarkable number of books and essays, filling countless notebooks in the process.

In January 1889 in the Piazzo Carlo Alberto in Turin, he watched as a cab driver beat his horse. Something in him snapped. Nietzsche flung himself around the horse's neck and eventually collapsed, utterly insane. He spent the following eleven years in a Basel asylum or in the care of his mother, until her death in 1897, and finally his sister, Elisabeth Förster-Nietzsche. He never recovered. It is suspected that Nietzsche suffered from syphilitic lunacy. If this were not degradation enough, Nietzsche's sister did much to squander her brother's legacy, and it is possible that her efforts had something to do with the disastrous appropriation of his philosophy by the Nazis. It is clear, though, that Nietzsche himself would have despised all of this. He certainly thought little of German nationalism in particular and party politics in general.

Truth and Values

It is not possible to work through Nietzsche's many volumes in any detail here, but we can consider some of the themes that recur in several of them. Nietzsche's writings are sometimes mistakenly regarded as lessons in nihilism, the view that values have no justification or meaning. Some take it that Nietzsche argues for the claim that there are no moral standards, that truth has no value, and that religion is decadent or dying, and certainly Nietzsche says all of this or nearly says it. Nihilism, though, is not his conclusion; it's his starting point. He argues that the West's intellectual and interpretive scaffolding, its underlying concepts which we all use to arrive at judgments of value, can no longer sustain us. Perhaps it was possible for human beings, once, to buy into the idea that value has a basis in something beyond this world (say God or the Absolute), but no longer. We are on the verge of a spiritual crisis, and something new is needed to sustain us, otherwise we plummet into the horrors of nihilism or worse.

Nietzsche views this crisis with something approaching joy, because he sees in it a new kind of freedom, a freedom to find value for ourselves. His catchphrase for the crisis of value is "God is dead," and it is easy to hear the happiness in Nietzsche's voice when you read it. Consider this passage:

> In fact, we philosophers and "free spirits" feel ourselves irradiated as by a new dawn by the report that the "old God is dead"; our hearts overflow with gratitude, astonishment, presentiment, and expectation. At last, the horizon seems open once more, granting even that it is not bright; our ships can at last put out to sea in face of every danger; every hazard is again permitted to the discerner; the sea, *our* sea, again lies open before us; perhaps never before did such an "open sea" exist.

Nietzsche's treatment of moral value is instructive, an illustration of what he takes to be free-thinking in the light of the realization that the current conceptions of value are bankrupt. His discussion is philosophical, though some deny this, as well as philological, quasi-historical, and, at times, verging on psychoanalytical. By laying bare the alleged meaning and history of our moral values, Nietzsche hopes to undermine them, reveal them for what they really are, and replace them with something better.

It is very easy to lose one's way in all of this, owing principally to Nietzsche's style—clarity and argumentation is sometimes exchanged for rhetoric and good prose. Nietzsche calls himself an "immoralist," suggesting that he renounces all conceptions of morality, but in fact he only wishes to reject the West's present moral categories. He also says that the admirable person is "a creator of values," and some see in this a kind of radical relativism or egoism, the view that each individual ought merely to function according to their own notion of right and wrong, perhaps only look after their own interests. This is probably another misreading. In fact, Nietzsche is calling for us to return to the moral concepts held by the Ancient Greeks. Morality, for both Nietzsche and at least some of the Greeks, depends on human nature; in particular it is an expression of what is excellent in us. For Nietzsche, though, human nature is not universal—our natures are different, and it therefore follows that different people can find and follow different conceptions of excellence, different moralities.

Morality and the Will to Power

In saying all of this, Nietzsche makes a distinction between master-morality and slave-morality. In the former kind of morality, the nobles or ruling classes call what is best in themselves "good" (truthfulness, power, pride in oneself) and what they despise in those they rule "bad" (weakness, lies, timidity, insignificance). The slaves, and in particular those with a priestly impulse, see things differently. In their impotence, unable to exercise power of any sort on their masters, they invert master-morality. "Good" is now applied to weakness, meekness, suffering, and loss, as well as those qualities most needed by the weak: sympathy, humility, friendliness, and patience. "Evil" becomes a term of abuse leveled by the weak at the properties of the strong they most despise: their health, power, and strength. Nietzsche writes: "... the wretched alone are the good; the poor, impotent, lowly alone are the good; the suffering, deprived, sick, ugly alone are pious, alone are blessed by God ... and you, the powerful and noble, are on the contrary the evil, the cruel, the lustful, the insatiable, the godless to all eternity ..."

The "slave revolt" in morality, according to Nietzsche, has left us with a slave-morality, and in this strange historical moment of freedom, what is needed is something near a return to master-morality.

Man and Superman

The return is exemplified by the *Übermensch* (the Overman or Superman), that being which has overcome what has so far defined us as human, the now-crumbling system of value. Humanity,

Nietzsche is shown here (right) with his star pupil Paul Ree, and Lou Salome, in perhaps an ironic comment on Nietzsche's infamous remark, "Thou goest to woman? Forget not thy whip."

such as it is, is now something to be overcome, and the Overman is "the lightning out of the dark cloud of man," the new ideal at which to aim. Nietzsche labels as "human, all too human" the religious or transcendental hopes and illusions characterized by our current dying scheme of value: the belief that virtue consists in obeying the will of a dead God, that the fictitious rewards of the next life somehow excuse subjugation in this one, and so on. The Overman renounces all of this, carving out his place in the world according to his own will.

The notion of will—in particular, the will to power—determines much of Nietzsche's thinking. Some incautious remarks in some of his notebooks suggest that Nietzsche might have toyed with the thought that everything is will to power, that the will to power is the elementary force underlying all reality or the fundamental explanatory principle. It first appears in his published work as one drive among others, a striving for control, but it is clear that in the end Nietzsche thought it was much more than this. Nietzsche has his prophet, Zarathustra, asserting that all life is will to power. In later works, he calls it "a life-affirming drive," and it is possible to settle on the view that, at the very least, the will to power is a kind of brute tendency for self-assertion manifested in us all. Couple this interpretation with his remarks on what is good, and one can begin to make some sense of otherwise perplexing passages.

But in reading Nietzsche, we want more than just sense; what we're after is truth. If what Nietzsche is proposing is a new conception of morality, then it should have some advice in it, shouldn't it? It should give us some thoughts on how to live, some idea of what we ought to value, some conception of rightness and wrongness in action. It's all very well to say that some return to the Greeks is required, that we must find our own value, but without further advice, isn't this just empty bad air?

It is difficult to think along such lines without imagining Nietzsche shaking with rage at the very thought of such an objection. His point is that human beings have had enough advice, enough listening, enough following. If we are to overcome the very herd instincts that motivate this kind of objection, we are going to have to do some thinking for ourselves.

MAJOR WORKS

The Birth of Tragedy (1872)
This recasts Greek culture in terms of wild Dionysian energy, rather than sober Apollonian reserve. Nietzsche sees in such energy the possibility of creative, cultural, and spiritual rebirth.

Human, All-Too-Human (1878)
A collection of usually pithy but sometimes perplexing aphorisms on an enormous range of topics. Here, the notion of power makes a genuine appearance in Nietzsche's writings.

Thus Spoke Zarathustra (1883–85)
A work among Nietzsche's most important writings. It recounts the development of Zarathustra, who prophesies the coming of the Superman and what might lie beyond the human condition.

Beyond Good and Evil (1886)
Nietzsche's account of morality, which also contains a mature expression of the will to power.

The Genealogy of Morals (1887)
It is possible to read this as a critique of Christian morality. It includes Nietzsche's account of the "slave revolt" in morality, as well as a blistering critique of the priesthood. It concludes with an expression of perspectivalism.

John Dewey

As well as a psychologist and progressive educational reformer, John Dewey (1859–1952) was one of the more influential American philosophers of the last century. With Peirce and James, he is associated with the pragmatic school of philosophy.

1859–1952

John Dewey (1859–1952) was born in Burlington, Vermont, on October 20, 1859, the third of the four sons of Archibald Dewey and Lucina Rich. He was brought up in modest circumstances. His father, a grocer, made a comfortable living, but was not particularly ambitious on behalf of his children, though he had a passion for Shakespeare and Milton and was in the habit of reciting Burns to his sons. He would have been quite content for them to have become tradesmen. Dewey's mother, twenty years younger than her husband, was, however, of different character; more intense and ambitious, and it was mainly at her urging that the three surviving boys—the eldest sibling having died in infancy—pursued college educations at the University of Vermont.

It was as an undergraduate that the seeds of Dewey's later intellectual commitments were first sown. Particularly, it was at this time that he came into contact with evolutionary thought, and the lessons he learned were to stay with him for the rest of his life. In the pre-modern world, species and organisms were seen as immutable, perfectly defined entities, the product of a benevolent designer. Darwin's theory blew this idea apart, showing that the natural world is in fact dynamic and fluid, and that organisms and species are ever-changing as they interact with their environment. This idea of iterative change became central to Dewey's conception of human nature. He rejected the idea that humans have a fundamental essence, and all that this involves in terms of the ends toward which their lives are directed, and the means employed to attain these ends, arguing instead that human beings are constituted in their interaction with the multiple aspects of their environment. Humans are through and through the product of a lived practice.

As a graduate student of psychology, Dewey became impressed with the scientific method

It wasn't only in the area of evolutionary thought that Dewey came to see the importance of a scientific way of thinking. As a graduate student at Johns Hopkins University, he came into contact with G. Stanley Hall, an experimental psychologist of international repute. Dewey was impressed with the power of the scientific method, and in his early writings he sought to reconcile it with Hegelian idealism. This, however, was not successful, and by the early 1890s, after he had taken up a position at the University of Chicago, he abandoned his idealism for the empirical, instrumental approach that he espoused for the next sixty years.

Dewey (center) espouses the creation of a liberal third party in U.S. politics at a convention of the League for Independent Political Action, 1932.

John Dewey

The Theory of Inquiry

At the center of this approach is his theory of inquiry, which aimed to show how thought emerges as people interact with their environments, and how the measure of true belief—or belief for which there is warranted assertability—is that it facilitates satisfactory responses to the circumstances that people confront, or, to put this another way, that it provides successful rules for conduct.

The best way of understanding this idea is first to consider what Dewey meant by the notion of "habit." As we have seen, he did not think that humans have a fixed, determinate nature. However, it is nevertheless the case that people tend to behave in fairly predictable ways. This is because they have learned, via the process of socialization, particular socially sanctioned habits. It is in this fashion that people are able to get by in their lives; they have adopted the modes of behavior that function to achieve specific goals in particular circumstances.

However, sometimes these habits break down; the actions and responses people can draw upon prove inadequate in terms of the situations they confront, and they cannot go on. It is at this point there appears the kind of genuine doubt that necessitates inquiry. In *How We Think* Dewey emphasized that this sort of doubt is not purely cognitive, not the doubt of a skeptical philosopher, it is *felt* doubt:

> In cases of striking novelty or unusual perplexity, the difficulty … is likely to present itself at first as a shock, as emotional disturbance, as a more or less vague feeling of the unexpected, of something queer, strange, funny, or disconcerting. In such instances, there are necessary observations deliberately calculated to bring to light just what is the trouble, or to make clear the specific character of the problem.

Having identified that there is a difficulty that needs addressing, in order to avoid the fairly ad hoc construction of possible solutions, the next stage in the process of inquiry is to isolate the significant elements of the problematic situation. Once this is achieved, then it is necessary to determine a number of hypotheses in order to solve the difficulty. This is a creative, imaginative process, and it involves going beyond what is given in the situation: "… it is more or less speculative, adventurous … it involves a leap, a jump, the propriety of which cannot be absolutely warranted in advance, no matter what precautions be taken" (*How We Think*).

The final stages in the process involve working through the implications of the various hypotheses that are being entertained, and then, crucially, testing them experimentally:

> Reasoning shows that if the idea be adopted, certain consequences follow. So far the conclusion is hypothetical or conditional. If we look and find present all the conditions demanded by the theory, and if we find the characteristic traits called for by rival alternatives to be lacking, the tendency to believe, to accept, is almost irresistible. (*How We Think*)

The resolution of this process involves the incorporation of new beliefs into the framework of habits, which allows people to act in concert with the events in their lives. Truth is that which works. For Dewey, then, it is a mistake to think, following Descartes, that the fundamental epistemological question is to do with how we can know that the stuff in our minds, our perceptions, corresponds with external reality. Rather, what counts is whether our beliefs provide us with rules of conduct that help us to interact with the world.

There is an important point here about the status of true beliefs, or, to adopt Dewey's terminology, "warranted assertions." Like Peirce, Dewey is committed to a fallibilistic epistemology. Beliefs constitute knowledge when they are confirmed by a community of genuine inquirers. However, the extent of the warrant varies, and all beliefs are subject to revision, not least because the circumstances in which problematic situations arise are changed by the very act of finding solutions to them.

Dewey extends his theory of inquiry into the moral domain. Just as he denied that there was an inviolate human essence, so he denied that there were absolute moral standards—whether they be handed down by religious or philosophic authority—that remain true even in changing circumstances. The goal of moral action then is not to

MAJOR WORKS

How We Think (1910)
This early work outlines Dewey's theory of inquiry; and suggests that beliefs will be adopted or rejected on the basis of their usefulness in allowing people to master the situations that they confront in their lives.

Democracy and Education (1916)
It represents the most systematic articulation of Dewey's ideas about education, stressing the importance of active, cooperative learning, and denying that education should be seen merely as preparation for civic and economic responsibilities. Also provides an interesting introduction to Dewey's more general philosophical ideas.

Human Nature and Conduct (1922)
This book seeks to establish a moral theory based on the study of human nature. Although this will not solve all moral problems, it is argued that it will allow them to be posed in such a way that it might be possible to work toward solving them.

The Public and Its Problems (1927)
This defends the ideal of participatory democracy against critics who had argued that the nature of modern societies precludes anything more than a severely restricted kind of democracy.

Logic: The Theory of Inquiry (1938)
Major statement of Dewey's pragmatism, and the theory of inquiry that underpins it.

conform to a given code of behavior, which would function merely to limit the expression of human potentiality, but rather to approach every situation with a view to constructing it in such a way that it offers the best opportunities for human fulfillment.

Value Judgments

This point can be illustrated by considering how value judgments work. For Dewey, value judgments are practical judgments; they guide the behavior we exhibit toward the things we value (our "valuings"). Value judgments come into play when our normal activity toward our valuings has been disrupted by a problematic situation—for example, I have found that I cannot get to sleep if I drink coffee late at night. The point of the value judgment—I ought to drink warm milk instead—is to enable one to adopt a new course of action, if required, in order to solve the problematic situation. Thus, value judgments are tools that function to help us to live better lives.

It is only possible to engage in this kind of moral reasoning if we cultivate the same habits of inquiry that are appropriate for finding out new things about the world. The measure of the appropriateness of a value judgment is how well it works in the world; that is, whether it results in consequences that we value as we hypothesized that we would—did I, in fact, sleep better having drunk warm milk rather than coffee before bed? Value judgments, then, like the judgments we make about things in the world, are subject to empirical verification. They are also necessarily provisional and revisable in the face of changing circumstances.

To accomplish scientific and moral reasoning in line with the precepts of Dewey's theory of inquiry requires that individuals are capable of flexible and sophisticated thought. There are clear implications here for the way that people should be educated. Particularly, Dewey argued that education should not be overly didactic in form; the idea is not simply to impart information that students will passively absorb. Rather, proper education aims to foster imaginative responses to new information and situations by engaging students in active, cooperative practices of learning. In this way, people develop the skills and habits required to enable them to function happily as full members of communities founded on principles of democratic participation.

John Dewey officially retired in 1930, but continued to teach as Professor Emeritus at the University of Columbia, where he had been working since 1904, until 1939. By this time, he was the preeminent figure in American philosophy. Even after he finished teaching, this was not the end of his philosophical and public activities. Most notably, he was the chairperson of the Commission of Inquiry which, on investigating the charges made against Leon Trotsky in the Moscow trials of the mid-1930s, found in favor of Trotsky and against Stalin.

Dewey died in 1952 at the age of 92. By this time, pragmatism was attracting less interest from professional philosophers. However, Dewey's place as a major figure in the philosophical firmament is assured. His criticisms of the classical tradition in Western philosophy remain pertinent today. He is a major influence in liberal, progressive thought. And moreover, there are today signs of a revival of interest in his ideas, particularly in the work of people like Richard Rorty and Jürgen Habermas.

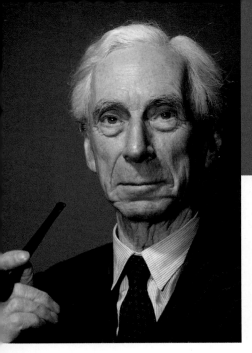

Bertrand Russell

Generally recognized as one of the founders of analytical philosophy, Bertrand Russell (1872–1970) is perhaps Britain's best-known, and most controversial, philosophical commentator of modern times.

1872–1970

Reflection on the life of Bertrand Russell, Third Earl Russell, can be a little tiring. He seems to have crammed a lot of living into a life that was unusually long. He probably did more than anyone in the first decades of the twentieth century to put philosophy on the course of logical analysis it generally still holds today. It equipped him with a method, and using it he came to large conclusions in the philosophy of mathematics, metaphysics, and epistemology. Without doubt, he was a brilliant mathematician, and according to some sources his insights into set theory had more than a little to do with the development of computing.

You might conclude from this that Russell was a wild-haired, desiccated calculating machine, detached from practical matters, but you would be quite wrong. Not only was he presentable and socially graceful, but he was an excellent stylist—he won the Nobel Prize for Literature in 1950—and his many public writings, particularly his *History of Western Philosophy* and *The Problems of Philosophy*, more often than not manage the rare combination of rigor and readability. He was also a very public figure, campaigning for civil rights and protesting against war and nuclear weapons, spending time in prison for his efforts. The story of his private life is a little darker and perhaps less admirable.

Russell was born in Trelleck, Monmouthshire, Wales, to Lord Amberley, oldest son of the First Earl Russell, and Kate Stanley, daughter of the second Baron Stanley of Alderly. His parents were dead by the time Russell was four years old, and this seems unusually tragic, both because he was then raised a little sternly by his austere, Unitarian grandmother and because Russell, by temperament, would have got on spectacularly well with his parents. He did not actually come to know much about them until he was eighteen, and it was probably with some delight that he discovered, as he writes with unconcealed pride in the first sentence of "My Religious Reminiscences," that they were "considered shocking in their day on account of their advanced opinions in politics, theology and morals."

Lord Amberley, for example, got himself thrown out of Parliament when it was discovered that he supported the use of birth control. Lady Amberley, for her part, spoke publicly in defense of women's suffrage,

Along with G.E. Moore, Russell led the revolt against "British Idealism," grounding his arguments in logic and mathematics

somehow managing to annoy Queen Victoria, who allegedly fumed, "I wish I could whip that Kate Amberley." The Amberleys were long-standing admirers of Bentham and Mill, and eventually became friends with the latter, contemplating the possibility of asking Mill to be the secular equivalent of Russell's godfather. Given his parents' early death, it is hard not to wonder what sort of philosopher Russell might have become had things turned out differently. A young Russell tutored at Mill's knee is an image it is difficult to clear from one's mind.

Russell took a place at Trinity College, Cambridge, to study mathematics, eventually turning to philosophy. He was appointed lecturer at Trinity, but his loud and public opposition to World War I led to his dismissal and, eventually, a prison term. He was reappointed but finally resigned from Trinity, becoming dependent on popular writings for an income. He remained politically active throughout his life, well into his nineties, campaigning against the United States' involvement in Vietnam and serving as a vocal proponent of the Campaign for Nuclear Disarmament.

Russell's life was also marked by a number of turbulent marriages and disastrous love affairs, suggesting that his capacity for clear-headed thinking somehow deserted him in the private sphere. His allegedly stunted capacity for emotion, which does not quite square with the occasional fervor of his public campaigns, is taken as the fundamental explanatory principle required for an understanding of Russell's personality by some biographers. It is hard to know just what to think in this connection.

The Revolt against Idealism

When Russell came of age at Trinity, the final stages of an intellectual shift in British philosophy from empiricism to variations on the idealisms of Kant and Hegel were being articulated by F.H. Bradley. In *Appearance and Reality*, Bradley operates with a modification of the Kantian distinction between the mind-constituted world of appearances and the world as it is in itself. The distinction is roughly between propertied objects standing in causal relations to one another in space and time on the one hand and reality itself on the other, which Bradley takes to be something akin to the Hegelian Absolute, a single Cosmic Experience of which we are a small, self-conscious part. Odd tenets follow from the view. For example, the very idea of independently existing things (bacon sandwiches and plates) standing in relations to one another (the bacon sandwich is on the plate) is incoherent. Reality itself is unified, and the appearance of distinct objects, as well as relations between them, is illusory. "Truths" about particulars, on this view, can only be partial.

Along with G.E. Moore, Russell led the revolt against British Idealism. While Moore deployed arguments rooted in common sense and ordinary language, Russell's arguments were grounded in logic and mathematics, the so-called "logical-analytic method." By expanding the scope of logic dramatically, along with A.N. Whitehead in the monumental *Principia Mathematica*, Russell shows that it is possible to restate propositions in a more rigorous and revealing logical form. This can sometimes uncover errors—such as vagueness, equivocation, or other sorts of confusions—in our everyday and philosophical talk. In addition to this and in direct reply to the idealists, Russell hoped to find a way to make talk of concrete particular objects, their properties and relations, logically respectable and clear, showing up confusions in idealist arguments in the process. The result was devastating to idealism, which more or less died the death in the English-speaking world, and it put logical analysis at the center of twentieth-century philosophical thinking.

Although Russell's various positions changed throughout his life—he made no apology for this, claiming that mental stagnation was far worse than the occasional revision of philosophical doctrine—he applied the same method to virtually all of the largest philosophical questions going. It might be that the method is more important than the answers he gives. He characterizes his view of the process in this passage:

> It seems to me that philosophical investigation, as far as I have experience of it, starts from that curious and unsatisfactory state of mind in which one feels complete certainty without being able to say what one is certain of. The process that results from prolonged attention is just like that of watching an object approaching through a thick fog … It seems to me that those who object to analysis would wish us to be content with the initial dark blur.

Even if we place a higher value on Russell's method than the content of his thinking, this is to take nothing away from that content. There is no question that the content has had large implications for the philosophy of mathematics, epistemology, and metaphysics.

The Problem of the External World

Consider Russell's response to the problem of how we know the nature of objects in the external world. Russell begins with reflections on perceptual experience. We seem to see tables, chairs, and books in the room, but closer inspection reveals that we are not quite seeing what we normally take ourselves to see. We suppose, for example, that the table is brown, perhaps uniformly brown, brown all over. However, parts of the table reflect light differently, and if you move your head around you will notice that the reflective parts shift around too. The apparent shape of the table changes as well—from above it looks circular, but from the side it looks elliptical. Putting other heads, other points of view, into the equa-

MAJOR WORKS

Principia Mathematica (with A N Whitehead) (1910–13)
A massive, three-volume explication of Russell's theory of mathematics. It contains his important theory of types, as well as a defense of logicism, the view that mathematics is a part of logic.

The Problems of Philosophy (1912)
Still among the very best popular or introductory books of philosophy, this slim volume manages to combine philosophical integrity with a clear, readable style.

A History of Western Philosophy (1945)
This is probably Russell's best known work. It is a masterful treatment, a clear explication of the whole of Western Philosophy.

Bertrand Russell: Logic and Knowledge (1965)
A collection of some of Russell's most important essays. It contains his "Lectures on the Philosophy of Logical Atomism," the view that the world is made up of logical atoms—fleeting patches of color or snippets of sounds, predicates, relations, and the facts composed of these atoms.

tion complicates matters further. What then are we seeing when we claim to see a table? What's the real table? "… [T]he real table, if there is one, is not the same as what we immediately experience by sight or touch or hearing. The real table, if there is one, is not *immediately* known to us at all, but must be an inference from what is immediately known."

Russell calls the ever-shifting appearances "sense-data." It is sense-data that we immediately know, with which we are directly acquainted, and about which it is hard to think we might be wrong. What is needed is a connection between sense-data and objects, and here Russell admits that the view of objects as substances cannot stand. A new conception of objects as logical constructions built out of or inferred from sense-data is required. On at least one reading of Russell's view (and Russell's account changed over time), objects are sets or collections of perspectives. It is important to notice that this is saying something different and something less than that we infer the existence of an object (in the usual sense) on the basis of sense-data. Instead, Russell is claiming that the objects themselves are logical constructions, not substances out there causing sense-data, at least not in a straightforward sense.

You can wonder, maybe unkindly, what these constructions of perspectives are perspectives on, and in so wondering you might have made a syntactical error which a good student of logic might be able to clear up for you. You can also take it that Russell's claims, to have any meat on the bones at all, have to be a form of inferential realism, the view that the existence of objects, even logically constructed objects, is somehow inferred from sense-data. If this is the right interpretation, you can object in the same way everyone objects to this sort of view: it seems to make the table invisible, and that can't be right.

There is another, more general objection to Russell's views and method, an objection he considered himself. All of this seems to make philosophy a branch of science or logic, seems to rob philosophy of what is most attractive about it, the speculative freedom or playfulness attending philosophical reflection. Reducing philosophical problems to complex, dry logical or mathematical matters makes the world boring. If this is true, Russell says:

> … then it's not my fault, and therefore I do not feel I owe any apology for any sort of dryness or dullness in the world. I would say this too, that for those who have any taste for mathematics, for those who like symbolic constructions, that sort of world is a very delightful one, and if you do not find it otherwise attractive, all that is necessary to do is to acquire a taste for mathematics, and then you will have a very agreeable world …

Many philosophers since Russell have taken this advice, a few going much further than Russell in circumscribing the limits of philosophical reflection to a more narrow range than even Russell would have liked. Still, the philosophical world as it is, no doubt because of the emphasis on logic in Russell's writings, would be a very agreeable world to him.

Russell was nothing if not a passionate, committed philosopher. Here he addresses a crowd in Trafalgar Square at an anti-nuclear weapons rally.

Ludwig Wittgenstein

Many people believe that Ludwig Wittgenstein (1889–1951) was the twentieth century's most important philosopher. It is somewhat ironic, then, that he is probably best known for waving a poker at fellow philosopher Karl Popper.

1889–1951

The setting for this peculiar event was a meeting of the Cambridge Moral Science Club in October 1946. There are different accounts of precisely what took place, but the general gist of it is that in the midst of a heated discussion about the validity of moral rules, Wittgenstein picked up a poker, gesticulated with it in order to make a point, and then abruptly departed the scene. Popper is said to have subsequently given as an example of a moral rule that one should not threaten visiting lecturers with pokers.

Wittgenstein's biographers all agree, as this story suggests, that he was an intense, if compelling, personality. He was born in Vienna on April 20, 1889, the youngest child of Leopoldine and Karl Wittgenstein. His father was a rich and successful Austrian industrialist and enjoyed a position of some prominence in Viennese society. The Wittgenstein home was a center of cultural excellence; Brahms and Mahler were frequent visitors, and the young Wittgenstein was encouraged in these early years, particularly by his mother, to develop his own musical interests.

His formal education, however, was a little unorthodox. He did not attend school until he was fourteen, and then not very successfully. It was assumed that like his father he would become an engineer—indeed, he had shown some aptitude in this direction—so, having failed in his ambition to read physics at university, he went off to study engineering, first in Berlin and then in Manchester. It was while at Manchester that he became interested in philosophy; he had read and been impressed by Bertrand Russell's *Principia Mathematica*, and on the advice of Frege, with whom he had corresponded, he went to Cambridge in 1912 to study with Russell.

The Picture Theory of Meaning

Although it was immediately clear that he was a brilliant thinker, he only stayed in Cambridge for a short while, opting instead to travel. However, this was interrupted in 1914 by the start of World War I. Wittgenstein immediately joined the Austrian army, serving mainly on the eastern front. During this time, he worked on the manuscript of the book that would eventually become his first great work, *Tractatus Logico-Philosophicus*.

The *Tractatus* was eventually published in 1922 with the help of Russell. It is a short book, only seventy pages long, but Wittgenstein, for a while at least, seemed to believe that it solved all the genuine problems of philosophy. The book set out what is known as the picture theory of meaning. The world is constituted by a set of atomic facts. Propositions—for example, the cat is black—are logical pictures of actual or possible facts; in other words, propositions stand for possible states of affair of the world. If the state of affair picked out by a proposition obtains in the world, then the proposition is true. Thus, it was Wittgenstein's claim that the underlying logical structure of language mirrors the logical structure of the world.

It must be said that it is hard to be clear about Wittgenstein's argument unless one has a thorough grounding in the issues that informed the work on language and logic of people like Frege, Russell, and Whitehead. However, there is an interesting general point about Wittgenstein's argument in the *Tractatus*. It was his view that language allows things to be said clearly or not at all: "What can be said at all can be said clearly, and what we cannot talk about we must pass over in silence."

Moreover, language marks the limits of thought; therefore, if it isn't possible to say something clearly, it isn't possible to think it without falling into nonsense. Part of the significance of this argument is that it led Wittgenstein to the thought that philosophy is a highly circumscribed endeavor. It is mainly about policing the limits of language; ensuring that we don't fall into the error of mistaking nonsense for meaning. Indeed, Wittgenstein famously said at the end of the *Tractatus*: "My propositions serve as elucidations in the following way: anyone who understands me eventually recognizes them as nonsensical."

Nonsensical or not, Wittgenstein took his cue from the publication of the *Tractatus* to give up philosophy for a while. He disappeared to Austria, where he took a job as a schoolteacher. This was not an entirely successful endeavor. There were accusations of almost tyrannical teaching practices —including an alleged incident of violence toward a female student—and eventually he gave up teaching to become a gardener at a monastery. At this point, something interesting happened. Wittgenstein began to talk with some of the members of the Vienna circle group of philosophers, in particular with Moritz Schlick, and he came to the view that perhaps the *Tractatus* had not solved all the genuine philosophical problems after all.

For a large class of cases ... the meaning of a word is its use in the language

This reassessment led to the second phase of Wittgenstein's philosophical career, in which he developed ideas that in many respects were completely at odds with his earlier philosophy. In particular, he came to believe that the idea that language is a determinate system, within which simple propositions stand for states of affairs of the world, was fundamentally misconceived. Rather, language is multifaceted and context-dependent; it is used for and accomplishes many different things. Thus, for example, it simply isn't possible to say how the phrase "I love you, too" will be understood unless the context in which it is said is known. To say it in response to an insult is to intend something entirely different than if it is said to a lover in a tender moment. Meaning is inextricably tied to the behavior of language users and the contexts in which they employ speech acts.

Philosophical Investigations

These new ideas about language and meaning were articulated most significantly in the posthumously published *Philosophical Investigations*. In this work, Wittgenstein set out to show that language gains its meaning from the way in which it is used: "For a *large* class of cases—though not for all—in which we employ the word 'meaning' it can be defined thus: the meaning of a word is its use in the language."

Linked to this idea is the notion of a "language-game"; the ways and contexts in which words are used depends upon the "game" being played. The idea of the language-game brings into focus the fact that language is linked to specific activities, or particular "forms of life." Wittgenstein mentioned as examples the following: giving orders and obeying them; reporting an event; speculating about an event; putting together a hypothesis; joke-telling; cursing; and storytelling. Much of *Investigations* is concerned with flagging the differences within and between various language games.

A Private Language

Wittgenstein in New York.
From a series of screenprints
based on Wittgenstein's life and
writings by Eduardo Paolozzi

Perhaps the most talked about section of *Investigations* is where Wittgenstein argued against the possibility of a private language. The argument is not presented in a standard way, with premises, deduction, and conclusions. Rather, in line with the style of the book as a whole,

it is constructed out of a series of short statements, with little explication of their meaning and intent. Consequently, there are many different interpretations of the private language argument; what follows, therefore, is just one particular interpretation.

Wittgenstein asks whether it is possible to "imagine a language in which a person could write down or give vocal expression to his inner experiences"—his feelings, moods, and the rest, where the "individual words of this language are to refer to what can only be known to the person speaking… So another person cannot understand the language."

To consider this possibility, he imagines the case where a person writes down "S" in a diary every time they experience a certain sensation. In this way, it seems possible to arrive at an ostensive private definition of "S"; every time the sensation occurs, and only when it occurs, the sign "S" is reproduced in thought or writing, thus establishing a permanent connection between "S" and the sensation, and thereby the meaning of the sign.

However, Wittgenstein identifies a problem with this argument. It isn't clear that we can ever establish the link between the sign "S" and the sensation in such a way so that on those occasions in the future where we employ the sign, we can be confident that we're using it correctly. In other words, in a private language there is no clear difference between remembering the correct application of a sign, and *believing* that one has remembered the correct application of a sign. As a result, the sign lacks meaning; nothing can ever establish that it is being used correctly. It follows, therefore, that a private language that refers to sensations is not possible; words gain their meaning from their use in a public context.

Although in his later work Wittgenstein largely came to reject the arguments that he had put forward in the *Tractatus*, it would be wrong to suppose that the discontinuity between his early and later periods was total. In particular, his view of the nature of philosophy remained constant. It was Wittgenstein's belief that the task of philosophy is to uncover and analyze the various ways in which we are befuddled and confused by language. As he put it in *Investigations*, philosophy "is a battle against the bewitchment of our intelligence by means of language."

Wittgenstein is one of the most interesting of the great philosophers. His work, of course, has been tremendously influential. It was, for example, directly implicated in the emergence of "ordinary language philosophy" after World War II. He is also interesting for reasons that are not directly to do with his philosophical output. His force of personality, for example, is renowned. He was a demanding, dramatic, and intense teacher. Many of the people who attended his seminars at Trinity College were afterward unable to imagine philosophy being conducted in any other way. He was also exceptional in the sense that he was *not* a scholar; he knew little of the standard texts of the philosophical canon, and indeed, he encouraged his students not to bother reading them. Yet he produced two distinct corpora of work, either of which would have been sufficient to establish his reputation as a great philosopher. It is easy to understand, then, how Bertrand Russell came to consider him to be perhaps the greatest intellect of his day.

MAJOR WORKS

Tractatus-Logico Philosophicus (1922)
The major work of Wittgenstein's early period, and a classic of twentieth-century philosophy. Outlines a picture theory of meaning, according to which meaningful propositions stand for particular states of affair of the world. A very short (20,000 words), yet hugely influential work, it was inspired by the writings of Frege, Russell, and Whitehead.

Philosophical Investigations (1953)
The most important work of Wittgenstein's later period, it represents a systematic expression of the ideas he came to hold about language and meaning. It includes an analysis of concepts such as "language-game" and "forms of life," and pursues the idea that words gain their meaning from the rules that govern their usage.

The Blue and the Brown Books (1958)
Although posthumously published, these books originate from the mid-1930s. They were dictated by Wittgenstein to his students, and constitute a useful introduction to the ideas of his later period.

On Certainty (1969)
A collection of writings on epistemology—knowledge and certainty—from the last few years of Wittgenstein's life. Primarily sourced from his notebooks.

Martin Heidegger

It was in the nature of nineteenth-century German philosophers to tackle the big questions, of God, time, and being, head on. Martin Heidegger (1889–1976) was one of the more successful.

1889–1976

A fallacy is an error of reasoning. Perhaps the most common one is the fallacy of *argumentum ad hominem* (argument to the man). An *ad hominem* is an argument directed not at the truth of a person's premises or the quality of their reasoning, but at the person themselves. It nearly goes without saying that a perfect villain can produce a fine piece of argumentation. A thug can say something true. Pointing out that a person is a villain does nothing to undercut the truth of their conclusions. Let us try to keep this logic primer firmly in mind throughout this consideration of the philosophy of Martin Heidegger. Some won't find this easy.

Heidegger was born in a small village in the Black Forest region of Germany, the eldest of the two sons of Friedrich and Johanna Heidegger. He had a religious impulse and tried to become a Jesuit but was refused on the grounds of ill health. He took up the study of theology, physics, mathematics, and philosophy at the University of Freiburg, where he came under the influence of the writings of Husserl. His studies were interrupted by World War I and brief service in the army. He was discharged within a year despite swift promotion, again for health reasons. He earned his doctorate with a thesis on the relation between psychology and philosophy, eventually working as a lecturer in philosophy at Freiburg, receiving modest payment for teaching from tuition fees.

> *Heidegger's project was nothing less than to uncover and rethink Being in its proper light*

Husserl took a post at the University of Freiburg, and Heidegger became his protégé, eventually breaking with Husserl's epistemology and method and striking out on his own. The result was *Being and Time*, and the book's success and Husserl's retirement afforded Heidegger the opportunity to take an excellent post at the university. He became its rector in 1933.

He also joined the National Socialist Party. He attended Nazi social gatherings in full socialist regalia. In his inaugural address, "The Self-Assertion of the German University," Heidegger went on a little about the spiritual mission of the people, the true destiny of Germany, and the role of the new rector in guiding the students and staff in the greater glorification of the German people. In a later speech, he told his students that "the Führer alone is the present and future German reality and its law." He reported to the authorities what he took to be the inappropriate thinking of several students and faculty members.

Following the war, the Freiburg Denazification Committee found that Heidegger held a prominent position in the Nazi Party and had incited students against some of his colleagues. He was stripped of his teaching post, pensioned off, and forbidden to teach until 1951. Heidegger spent some time in an asylum. He was eventually reinstated as Professor Emeritus but never taught in Germany again. Despite the urgings of prominent friends, Herbert Marcuse among them, Heidegger never commented publicly on or apologized for his activities during the war.

The Question of Being

Being and Time is an unusual and original book, dealing as it does with a peculiar question, what Heidegger calls "the question of being." It is Heidegger's contention that philosophical and everyday thinking somehow obscures the true nature of what it is for something to exist, and his project is to uncover and rethink being in its proper light. It is his view that the Presocratic philosophers were somehow genuinely in touch with or had the right conception of being, which philosophy has since managed to bury and obscure. His efforts consist in part in recovering this ancient conception. The largest part of the problem is conceptual, and this manifests itself in misleading talk about being. The solution involves us in neologisms, which some find unduly obscurantist. Perhaps some charity is required here. If Heidegger is right, and

Heidegger (right, marked with "X"), is shown here at a Nazi party meeting at the University of Freiburg, where he served as rector throughout World War II.

Martin Heidegger

the language we use clouds an honest grasp of his subject matter, what else can he do but coin new words or use old words in unusual ways?

One such word is "Dasein," translated variously as "the entity that each of us himself is" or "being-in-the-world." The bare term is used so as to beg no questions, presuppose no notion of person or human being beyond whatever it is that we are. Coming to grips with the nature of being, Heidegger seems to suppose, requires a consideration of a certain sort of being, us, for whom the question "What is being?" is a fundamental or at least a component part of its nature.

Philosophical misconceptions of the nature of human being abound. Thus Heidegger: "… all conventional, objectifying representations of a capsule-like psyche, subject, person, ego, or consciousness in psychology and psychopathology must be abandoned in favor of an entirely different understanding. The new view of the basic constitution of the human being may be called Dasein or being-in-the-world."

Martin Heidegger is pictured here in traditional Bavarian dress, after World War II. Heidegger's refusal to apologize for his support for Hitler during the Nazi period resulted in his suspension from teaching from 1945 until 1950.

What is a Person?

Consider Descartes's conception of a person as consisting in the intimate union of two distinct substances, one mental and the other physical. We take it that the world of objects is a physical world, but then what to do with the part of us that is mental? If a human being is conceived as one part bodily, an object like any other in the world, and one part mental, a thinking thing entirely unlike physical objects, our fundamental place within the world is thus obscured. In particular, our nature as being-in-the-world, things with an intimate concern with the world, is somehow neglected. The Cartesian view disconnects us from physical reality.

A large part of the project thus entails a fleshing out of the fundamental features of Dasein, a reconceptualization of whatever it is that we are which takes account of our relation to the world. Heidegger identifies three such features: factuality, existentiality, and fallenness.

Features of Dasein

Dasein is, in a sense, already here. A part of the human condition, which Heidegger calls our "factuality," consists of being thrown in the world, abandoned as it were by some past disaster to a life raft, being already a part of the ongoing show. It is possible to have the experience of just waking up in the middle of a life, recognizing that one is where one is as a result of past facts or decisions over which one now has no control. This is the factuality of Dasein, and it consists in the fact that Dasein has a past through which it is somehow constituted in the present.

Dasein, despite being partially determined by the past, also has a feeling of freedom with respect to the future. Dasein is not just constituted by its fixed past but also by its open, possible future, and the responsibility that attends this. This is the existentiality of Dasein, and it pulls in the opposite direction of factuality, not back to the past but forward into the future.

If the genuine self consists partly in the recognition of both past determinants and future possibilities, the third feature of Dasein, fallenness, identifies the human capacity to ignore both past and future. As a being in the world, Dasein loses itself in the mundane concerns of the present moment. Past and future horizons shrink to a present vanishing point. It is a simple fact of humanity that we neglect large parts of our nature, our past and future, embedding ourselves in the daily grind. We really do measure out our lives with coffee spoons.

It should be clear by now that the nature of being, as revealed by this consideration of the nature of Dasein, is bound up with time. Coming to a recognition of this is part of Heidegger's answer to the question of being. He writes: "Temporality temporalizes itself fully in each ecstasy, i.e. in the ecstatic unity of the complete temporalizing of temporality there is grounded the wholeness of the structural complex of existentiality, factuality, and fallenness, which comprises the unity of the care-structure."

Some might not find the language helpful, but the point is that human time in its entirety requires careful consideration if we are to understand the true nature of being. We have to do better than our current preoccupation with the present. In addition to having a past and a present, human time is essentially a time with a limit. The true meaning of Dasein consists partly in the recognition of past determinants and present concerns, but also in being alive to future possibilities. It requires being alive to one inescapable future possibility in particular: being dead. The authentic self brings its many temporal relations into a kind of unity, in light of past, present, and a limited future, and acts in the world on this basis.

The concept of "Dasein" is translated variously as "the entity that each of us himself is" or "being-in-the-world"

There is no question of Heidegger's large influence on recent thinking, particularly on the philosophy of continental Europe. Certainly he had an effect on Sartre and the existentialist movement in philosophy, although he was at pains to distance himself from it. The current preoccupation with deconstruction, in particular in the hands of Jacques Derrida and some feminist philosophers, but also as a form of literary criticism, is certainly owed to Heidegger. Marxists and social critics of nearly every sort find in Heidegger grist for various mills. Heidegger wrote a great deal following his suspension from teaching, much of which has still to be published and translated into English. Given this if nothing else, it is likely that Heidegger's true importance in the history of philosophy has not yet been realized.

MAJOR WORKS

Being and Time (1927)
This is Heidegger's most impressive work. It was his first work of any academic significance, and secured him a full professorship at Marburg University. It is a long, highly technical (some might say obscurantist) analysis of human nature and its fundamental connection to time. It introduces the concept of Dasein, "being-in-itself," and attempts to discover the essence of this being.

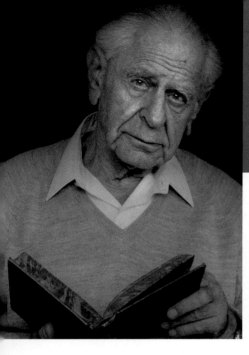

Sir Karl Popper

Sir Karl Popper (1902–94) is certainly among the most influential philosophers of science in the twentieth century, as well as an important critic of Marxism, but his reputation is still under consideration.

1902–94

Inductive inference moves from a number of particular observations of types of thing, to a general conclusion about things of that type

Reasonable people disagree about the real importance of Popper, about his actual standing in the history of philosophy. Enthusiasts hold well-attended Popper Conferences, identifying him as the Philosopher of the Century. His loudest detractors point to large muddles in his allegedly best work and make sport of some of Popper's incautious claims about the mind and the objectivity of theories, made late in life. Cooler heads withdraw from the debate, maintaining that we are too close in time to Popper's life and leave it to future philosophers to come to conclusions about his standing. We'll join the ranks of the last group in the following paragraphs.

Popper was raised in Vienna following World War I, and the times made a formidable impression on him. Although he was the son of a well-to-do lawyer, he witnessed poverty and political upheaval at first-hand. It moved him enough for him to undertake social work. He helped in a clinic for neglected children operated by the Freudian Alfred Adler, and it is clear that some of the events during this part of his life had an influence on his later philosophy. Probably it motivated his thesis topic; certainly it had an effect on his conception of what distinguishes science from other activities like psychoanalysis.

He became a socialist and then a communist. Following the deaths of student and worker protesters at the hands of police, at least some of Popper's communist acquaintances argued that the deaths were a help to the cause. Popper had different views about the value of human life and the ends of political action. The experience led to his rejection of communism and to his eventual critique of Marxism.

He attended the University of Vienna, earning a PhD with a thesis on the nature of method in psychology, as well as a qualification to teach mathematics and physics in secondary school. While working as a teacher in schools, his thesis caught the eye of several members of the Vienna Circle—a group of philosophers, mathematicians, physicists, and others who were instrumental in the logical positivist movement in the 1920s and 30s. Popper became a contributor to the Circle's discussions, and members of the group would eventually help Popper publish his first book, *The Logic of Scientific Discovery*. The book was read widely, and as a consequence Popper was invited to lecture at universities both in the United States and Great Britain.

Popper's parents, both from Jewish families, converted to Lutheranism in the hope of blending into Viennese society and had Popper baptized in the faith. Nevertheless, Popper was regarded as Jewish by the Nazis. His British colleagues had a great deal to do with helping Popper out of Vienna and into a philosophy post at University College, Christchurch, New Zealand. Popper remained there throughout World War II, teaching and producing his "war work": *The Poverty of Historicism* and *The Open Society and Its Enemies*. Following the war, he took a post at the London School of Economics, where he continued to defend his views on the nature of science, politics, and epistemology. We'll now consider a part of his philosophy of science.

The Problem of Induction

Since Hume, philosophers have been lumbered with the problem of induction. Inductive inferences move from a number of particular observations, where several instances of a type of thing have been observed to possess a certain sort of property, to a general conclusion about all things of that type—whether we have seen them or not. Hence the predictive power associated with induction. This snail eats lettuce; so does this one; and this one; and this one too. So, all snails eat lettuce. I bet the next one I find eats lettuce. Inductive inferences seem supported by a principle of this form: if a very large number of things have been observed under all sorts of different conditions, and every one of them has had a certain kind of property, then all such things have that property. As Hume shows, this principle cannot be justified on either logical or experiential grounds, and those seem to be the only justificatory games in town.

The worrying fact for the philosophy of science is that science seems to proceed on inductive grounds. It's not just our knowledge of snails, but a very large body of what we take to be paradigmatically justified knowledge, scientific knowledge, knowledge rooted in the rigors of scientific experimentation, that seems jeopardized by the problem of induction. If science depends on induction, and induction has no rational justification, is scientific inquiry therefore irrational? If so, and if you want to find a cure for cancer, why not consult an astrologer instead of a scientist? It's probably cheaper.

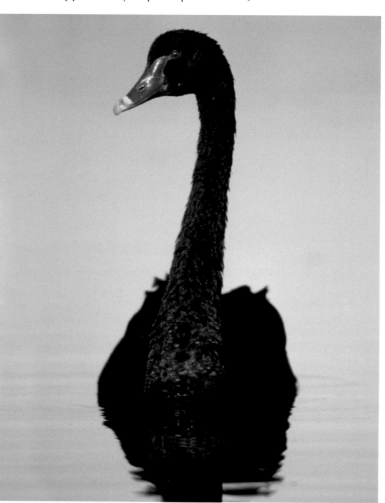

According to the principle of falsifiability, the proposition "all swans are white" can never be proven; a single instance of a black swan, however, can serve to falsify it.

We have here the two problems that Popper hopes to solve. In what does the rationality of science consist? What distinguishes science from other enterprises?

Popper attempts to avoid the problem of induction by arguing that scientific rationality consists in the falsification of theories, not the inductive verification of them. The view is based on a neat logical asymmetry. As we've just seen, you can observe as many snails as you like, but still your general theory that all snails eat lettuce will remain unproven. However, if you view just one snail that refuses to eat lettuce, you have produced a disproof of the general theoretical claim. It may be logically impossible to prove the truth of a theory by observation, but just one negative observation is enough to falsify a theory.

Falsifiable Hypotheses

Popper views scientific endeavor as the tentative proposal of hypotheses or conjectures that aim to describe some part of the world or solve some problem, followed by the vigorous attempt to falsify them with experimentation. Not just any general statement or theory counts as a scientific one. Given his views on scientific rationality, Popper argues that science works with falsifiable hypotheses, statements, or sets of statements that might be undermined by observation, and this is part of what distinguishes science from other activities.

The point about Freudian theory is that it is not falsifiable; it has no negative empirical consequences

Some hypotheses are obviously not falsifiable on logical grounds—for example, there's no experimental test that could show that "Either snails eat lettuce or they don't" is false. However, other instances of nonscientific hypotheses are a little more subtle. Suppose I tax you with my Freudian view that unconscious fears of a father figure actuate human behavior. A little exasperated, you demand some empirical evidence. We go to a tavern to observe human interactions, and spot a man hesitating to assert himself at the bar. I explain this easily as evidence that my theory is correct: the man is afraid of the barman; he sees him as a father figure and fears him; hence his hesitation. On the other hand, had the man banged his fist on the bar, demanding the barman's attention, my theory could accommodate this just as easily: the man is attempting to overcome his fear of the barman, a father figure, by asserting himself.

The point is that the Freudian theory is not falsifiable; it has no negative empirical consequences. Thus, for Popper, it is no piece of science. On the contrary, good science consists in bold conjectures, which make a difference to how our observations ought to turn out. Thus Popper:

> I can therefore gladly admit that falsificationists like myself much prefer an attempt to solve an interesting problem by a bold conjecture, *even (and especially) if it soon turns out to be false*, to any recital of a sequence of irrelevant truisms … in finding that our conjecture is false we shall have learnt much about the truth and shall have got nearer the truth.

You may rightly begin to smell a rat here. Is the claim really that scientists do or ought to try to undermine theories? It is hard to imagine scientists getting the champagne out on the discovery of an observation that conflicts with their pet theory, particularly if they have families to support and reputations to uphold. A number of objections to Popper deny that he has managed to describe or prescribe science in the right way—perhaps he has failed to take account of the social aspect of the scientific endeavor.

The Aim of Science

Further, science has practical aims; in the spirit of Bacon, we hope that science can improve human life, serve as a basis for choosing and believing. But if we can never know whether or not a theory is true, as Popper has it, then how do we know which of our currently not-yet-falsified theories is the best guide for action? Popper's answer is a little unnerving: theories that have survived ruthless testing should guide us. Unless we fall back into induction, though, we have no reason to think this is true.

It gets much worse, particularly when we carry on thinking about actual situations. First of all, scientific theories are not merely sentences about snails but sometimes vast structures supported by a number of auxiliary hypotheses. Testing situations, too, depend on additional theory, not least theory concerning the proper functioning of equipment, the precise nature of the initial conditions for experimentation. If a falsifying result occurs, one can locate the fault anywhere in a huge pile of theoretical claims and assumptions, keeping the kernel of the theory in place no matter what. If you do not get the result you were hoping for, maybe the machines need recalibrating.

Some argue that observation statements themselves are theory-laden. This is to say that all observations depend on some theory, even very low-level theory. Popper admits this, arguing that observation-statements, like theoretical statements, are themselves tentative, accepted by convention, and susceptible to testing too. He writes:

> The empirical basis of objective science has thus nothing "absolute" about it. Science does not rest upon solid bedrock. The bold structure of its theories rises, as it were above a swamp. It is like a building erected on piles. The piles are driven down from above into the swamp, but not down to any natural or "given" base.

Does it make sense to think of theories as things that can be falsified, given all of this? Some think it does, and Popper is not without an army of supporters who continue his work.

MAJOR WORKS

The Logic of Scientific Discovery (1935)
Sets out the doctrine of falsificationism, the view that science proceeds not by induction, but by the deductive demonstration of the falsity of scientific theory. The second part of the work deals with theories, testing, probability, quantum theory, and the nature of corroboration.

The Open Society and Its Enemies (1945)
This is Popper's major work in the philosophy of social science. It is a work in two volumes; the first volume is aimed at Plato, specifically his idea of "philosopher-kings" as the ideal rulers. The second volume deals with Karl Marx. It attempts to explain the rise of totalitarianism and says what ought to be done about it.

Conjectures and Refutations (1963)
Carries on the work of both earlier books, expanding on various falsificationist principles and applying them not just to the philosophy of science but to political philosophy as well.

Jean-Paul Sartre

Jean-Paul Sartre (1905–80) is the philosopher whose work—certainly in the English-speaking world—came largely to define the existentialist movement in the twentieth century.

1905–80

The image of the existentialist as a café-dwelling, chain-smoking, beret-wearing, intellectual type comes largely from Sartre. And the themes he explored in his writings—particularly the primacy of individual existence, human freedom, and the lack of objective values—are precisely those of existentialism.

Sartre was born into a comfortable, middle-class existence. However, his childhood was far from happy. He was brought up in the home of his maternal grandfather, Karl Schweitzer—a strict and domineering man—his father having died when he was just one year old. He was an unattractive child, short in stature and the victim of an eye condition that made it appear as if his gaze were permanently askance. He had few childhood friends, and spent most of his early life reading and writing in his grandfather's library. There was also a strange dynamic between Sartre and his mother; until his grandfather eventually put an end to it, she pampered him, dressed him in ornate clothing, and let his hair grow long.

However, whatever his childhood difficulties, it was clear from very early on that Sartre was extremely smart. Or as he put it, he was a child prodigy (though apparently not able to spell too well). Of course, we now know that the prodigy grew up to be one of the most celebrated intellectuals of the twentieth century. Sartre is perhaps unique in the extraordinary breadth of his accomplishments. As well as being a considerable philosopher, he was also a top-flight novelist, playwright, and biographer. Indeed, in 1964 he was offered the Nobel Prize for Literature, which he declined, saying that he didn't want to be "transformed into an institution."

Being and Nothingness

In the case of Sartre, there is something paradoxical in wondering whether his childhood explains the kind of life he lived as an adult, because Sartre is the consummate philosopher of freedom. He did not think, at least not in any uncomplicated way, that people are condemned to live certain kinds of lives by the events that occur in their past. Indeed, it is a common view about Sartre that he is a kind of radical humanist, concerned with the requirement that individuals face to choose their own lives and the morals that they espouse. However, although there is something right about this view, the truth about Sartre's philosophy is more strange than might at first be supposed.

Some of this strangeness derives from how he conceptualized consciousness and the human subject. In *Being and Nothingness* (1943), his major existential work, Sartre divided being into two primary realms: being for-itself, which is consciousness; and being in-itself, which is everything else. He argued that the for-itself is characterized by *nothingness*—that is, emptiness lies right at the heart of being. What did he mean by this? In simple terms, he meant that there is no human essence. Consciousness is permanently detached from the given order of things. It is pure, empty possibility, and therein lies its freedom.

This is a complicated idea. Some light can be shed on it by considering Sartre's treatment of the concept of *negation*. This concerns the capacity to conceive of what is not the case. It is manifest in a whole series of attitudes that the for-itself can adopt toward the objects to which it is directed. Perhaps most significant is the ability of the for-itself to project beyond the given present to an open future of unrealized possibilities—to imagine what *might* be the case. In this sense, the freedom of the for-itself is the permanent possibility that things might be other than they are. Human beings do not find this freedom easy to live with. With the realization that the future is always radically

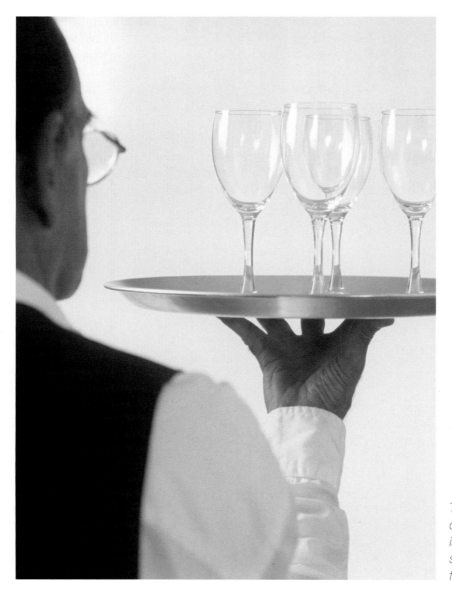

To identify oneself in the role of "waiter," Sartre maintains, is an example of bad faith; a subsumation of one's absolute freedom within an adopted role.

in doubt comes *anguish*. Sartre argued that in order to escape anguish, individuals adopt strategies of *bad faith*, that is, they seek to deny the freedom that is inevitably theirs.

Bad Faith

There are a couple of very famous examples that illustrate this point. Sartre asked us to imagine a liaison between a woman and a man who she knows wants to seduce her. He takes her hand, but rather than facing up to the requirement to accept or reject him, the woman pretends not to notice; she leaves her hand there as if she were just a passive object. In this way, by, as it were, denying her own subjectivity, she avoids the obligation to choose. The second example involves an over-zealous café waiter who plays his role with just a bit too much care. Sartre's idea here is that the waiter is attempting to subsume himself within his role; to make it as if everything he says and does is determined by his "waiterhood." Of course, for Sartre the reality is quite different. The man chose to be a waiter, and at every instance he makes the choice again, because no person has the kind of identity that the waiter seeks in his waiterhood.

A kind of bad faith can also enter into the way that people think about matters of morality. For example, individuals can attempt to flee the freedom that is theirs by adopting an attitude of *seriousness* toward a perceived moral sphere. That is, they might portray their actions as entirely governed by a binding moral code: "I'd like to help you, but I *can't*, it would be wrong." Of course, as far as Sartre is concerned, this is just so much rationalization. In his popular *Existentialism and Humanism*, he considers the case of a young man who is confused about whether or not to join the French Free Forces to fight the Germans or whether to stay at home to look after his mother. He shows that it is very difficult to see that there are any clear guides to action in such a situation. Christian ethics, for example, doesn't

MAJOR WORKS

The Transcendence of the Ego (1936)
This work develops a phenomenological account of the ego, which is specified as a construct rather than the indivisible source of a person's behavior and character.

La Nausee (1938)
Perhaps Sartre's major existentialist novel, in which he explores the philosophical implications of the contingency of existence through the experiences, charted in a diary, of its main character, Antoine Roquentin.

Sketch for a Theory of Emotions (1939)
In contrast to the traditional view, which sees emotions as largely unchosen, this work articulates the view that they are actively constructed in order to transform our experience of the world.

Being and Nothingness (1943)
Sartre's major work is primarily given over to an analysis of being-for-itself (or consciousness). It features groundbreaking discussion of anguish, bad faith, the spirit of seriousness, being-for-others, and other central elements of existentialism.

Existentialism and Humanism (1948)
Popular work in which Sartre defends existentialism against some of the criticisms that had been leveled against it. Features discussions of "abandonment" and the absence of an objective moral sphere.

Critique of Dialectical Reason (1960)
A Marxist makeover of existentialism. It represents a retreat from the existentialist emphasis on radical freedom, stressing instead the historical and social constraints on human choice.

offer any way of deciding between the general aim of fighting for the whole community and the precise aim of helping one particular person to live. Sartre concludes that all that it is possible to say is that the moral choices that individuals make are theirs and theirs alone, and they are fully responsible for them. All people can do is to choose authentically in the full recognition that they choose freely.

However, the fact that the for-itself is always and inevitably free does not mean that individuals make their choices in a vacuum. Rather, they face up to the specifics of the situations that they confront—for example, that the thief is carrying a knife—and the facticity of their particular lives. *Facticity* here refers to all the things about an individual that cannot be changed at any given point in time—for example, their age, gender, and genetic dispositions. Choices then are made against a particular background, so freedom of consciousness does not translate into the idea that people are free to do absolutely anything at the drop of a hat.

Human Freedom and the Self

Interesting in this regard is the role of the self and its relation to human freedom (the self was first properly discussed in an early work, *The Transcendence of the Ego*). Sartre denied that individuals have essential selves. Indeed, part of what defines his philosophy as existentialist is his claim that existence precedes essence. We exist first; the self that we subsequently become is a construct that is built and rebuilt out of experiences and behavior. In principle, then, the self is something that can be changed, it can be reconstructed. However, in practice, it is not easy to choose a course of action that is out of character with the *fundamental project* of the self. Consequently, the self that we have become imposes another limit on the practice of the freedom that belongs inevitably to the for-itself.

In this discussion of Sartre's ideas, we have concentrated on the philosophical foundations of his notion of freedom. As a result, his philosophy comes out looking as though it is almost entirely concerned with the individual. This is something of a distortion. It would have been possible to have entered Sartre's work at a different point—for example, with his later book, *Critique of Dialectical Reason*—and to have painted a different kind of picture. His commitment to Leftist politics, his interest in the dynamics of social groups, and the fact that he lived at a time of massive political and social upheaval meant that he was almost bound to move beyond the concerns of his early work. Indeed, by the 1960s, with the popularity of structuralism and the emergence of poststructuralism and postmodernism in continental Europe, Sartre's earlier existentialist philosophy had largely fallen into disrepute.

Fashion in intellectual circles is never constant, and there has been something of a revival of interest in Sartre's work

However, fashion in intellectual circles is never constant, and there has been something of a revival of interest in Sartre's work. Certainly, Sartre remained close to the heart of the French people right up until his death in 1980. His funeral in Paris was attended by more than twenty thousand people, and the crowds were so dense that his long-term partner Simone de Beauvoir was almost mobbed as she arrived at the cemetery. Twenty-five years later, people are still visiting his grave, now shared with de Beauvoir, to pay their respects.

Michel Foucault

Michel Foucault's (1926–84) influence extends beyond philosophy across the humanities and social science. He is perhaps best known for his critiques of various social institutions, most notably psychiatry, medicine, and the prison system.

1926–84

The British philosopher Ted Honderich once said of late twentieth-century French philosophy "that it aspires to the condition of literature or the condition of art"; that one thinks of it as "picking up an idea and running with it, possibly into a nearby brick wall or over a local cliff, or something like that." It is very easy to find examples of the kind of thing that Honderich is talking about. Here's Jacques Derrida defining the word "sign" in *Of Grammatology*: "… the sign is that ill-named thing, the only one, that escapes the instituting question of philosophy: 'what is …?'"

Yes, the crossings out are deliberate. The idea is that the erased words are inadequate to express their intended meaning, but that there aren't any better words either. So they are put "under erasure." David Lehman, in his book about deconstruction, *Signs of the Times*, says of this technique that it very quickly becomes an annoying affectation. Many people will agree with him.

Happily, not all modern French philosophy is quite so esoteric. The work of Michel Foucault is a case in point. It is true that in comparison with Paine and Mill, for example, Foucault is a difficult philosopher. However, he is no more difficult to understand than Kierkegaard, and he is considerably easier to get to grips with than Hegel. His work also has the merit that it has original and interesting things to say about power, knowledge, and subjectivity.

Foucault was born on October 15, 1926 in Poitiers, France, the second child of Anne Malapert and Paul Foucault, a prominent local surgeon and professor of anatomy. His father hoped and expected that his son too would choose to become a doctor. However, it seems that Foucault's family were not the formative influence they might have been. Rather, in an interview, Foucault suggested that his future ambitions were most profoundly affected by his experience of World War II; thus, in 1946, he entered the École Normale Supérieure, graduating in 1951 with degrees in philosophy and psychology. Foucault then went abroad for several years—according to some commentators, in order to escape the conservative mores of French culture—taking up teaching jobs in Sweden, Poland, and Germany, before returning to France in 1960 to join the philosophy department at the University of Clermont-Ferrand.

This marked the beginning of the period that established Foucault's intellectual reputation. In 1961, he published his first major work, *Madness and Civilization*; and he followed this up with eight further books written over a twenty-year period, which included *The Order of Things, The Archaeology of Knowledge, Discipline and Punish*, and *The History of Sexuality*.

Power and the Self

These works show Foucault mapping out a new course for French philosophy in the latter part of the twentieth century. He drew upon the disciplines of philosophy, history, psychology, and sociology in an attempt to show how power and knowledge interact to produce the human subject, or, the self. His intention was to demonstrate that human beings are constituted as knowing, knowable, as well as self-knowing subjects in relations of power and discourse, which necessitated rethinking the concept of power, and analyzing the links between power and knowledge.

Foucault claims that modern Western societies are characterized by three modes of objectification, which function to constitute human beings as subjects. These modes are: "dividing practices"; "scientific classification"; and "subjectification."

Dividing practices objectify people by distinguishing and separating them from their fellows on the basis of distinctions, such as normal and abnormal, sane and insane, the permitted and the forbidden. It is by means of dividing practices that people are categorized, for instance, as madmen, prisoners, and mental patients. These categories provide human subjects with the identities through which they will recognize themselves and be recognized by others. Thus, in *Madness and Civilization*, Foucault analyzed the mechanisms by which madness was established as a specific category of human behavior, one that legitimized the detention of individuals in institutions.

The mode of scientific classification objectifies by means of the discourses and practices of the human and social sciences. For instance, it is possible to break down mental illness into the numerous categories of the American Psychiatric Association's *Diagnostic and Statistical Manual of Mental Disorders*; in the *Birth of the Clinic*, Foucault showed how the emergence of the human sciences in the nineteenth century led to the human body being treated as an "object" to be analyzed, labeled, and cured, something still characteristic of modern medicine.

Subjectification is slightly different from the first two modes of objectification in that it refers to the way in which people actively constitute *themselves* as subjects. This idea runs through Foucault's *History of Sexuality*, where he analyzes how the desire to understand oneself leads to our confessing our most personal thoughts, feelings, and desires both to ourselves and to others. This necessarily implicates us in networks of power relations with authority figures—for example, doctors, psychiatrists and, in the twenty-first century, perhaps even TV producers—who maintain that they can understand our confessions and reveal the truth of them. It was Foucault's contention that through the expansion of this process of confession, people become objects of their own knowledge and of other people's knowledge; objects, moreover, who have learned how to reconstitute and change themselves. He argued that this phenomenon is a central part of the expansion of the technologies for the control and discipline of bodies and populations in modern societies.

The general process of the objectification of the human subject is linked to historical changes in the nature of power, and to corresponding developments in the areas of human and scientific knowledge.

Foucault used the expression "power/knowledge" to denote this conjunction of power and knowledge. Instead of focusing on coercion, repression, and prohibition, he showed how power *produces* human subjects and the knowledge we have of them. This idea has its fullest expression in the notion of "biopower."

Foucault noted that in the course of the seventeenth century, state power began to make its presence felt in all parts of a person's life; then, with the emergence of industrial capitalism, there was a move away from the use of physical force as a kind of negative power toward new, more effective, technologies of power, which were productive and aimed to foster human life. The state started to focus on the growth and health of its population. Foucault argued that a new regime of biopower had become dominant, which aimed at the management and administration of the human species or population, and the control or "discipline" of the human body.

State Power and State Control

In *Discipline and Punish* (1975), Foucault showed how Jeremy Bentham's idea of the panopticon, a type of prison, was a paradigmatic example of disciplinary technology. The panopticon is built in such a way that it functions effectively whether or not prison guards are actually present. Prisoners have no way of knowing whether they are being watched, and so they must behave as if surveillance were constant and never-ending. Effectively, then, prisoners become their own guardians. Thus, according to Foucault, the panopticon brings together power, knowledge, the control of the body, and the control of space into a single, integrated disciplinary technology. The parallels here with wider society are clear. Society exerts its greatest power to the extent that it produces individual

MAJOR WORKS

Madness and Civilization (1961)
An analysis of the genesis of modern psychology, it attacks the idea that "madness" and "mental illness" are natural categories, suggesting instead that they exist at the intersection of various institutional, social, and political imperatives.

Birth of the Clinic (1963)
This work, the first of Foucault's archeological studies, shows how the emergence of the human sciences, and medical science in particular, led to the human body being treated as an "object" to be analyzed, labeled, and cured.

The Order of Things (1966)
A complex analysis of the "epistemes"—the systems of thought and knowledge—which, across time, have underpinned various kinds of social scientific inquiry. It pursues the claim that different ages have a different understanding of the relations between language and truth.

The Archeology of Knowledge (1969)
A theoretical articulation of the archeological method which had underpinned his previous historical studies. A difficult book, it introduces the new concept of a discursive formation, which "presents the principle of articulation between a series of discursive events and other series of events, transformations, mutations, and processes."

Discipline and Punish (1975)
A study of the emergence of the modern prison, and, more generally, a disciplinary technology that functions to classify and control human subjects.

The History of Sexuality (three volumes, 1976, 1984, 1984)
These three volumes represent the beginnings of a study on human sexuality that Foucault never completed. The most mature expression of Foucault's thoughts about biopower and biopolitics.

human subjects who police themselves in terms of the discourses and practices of sexual, moral, physical, and psychological normality.

Foucault's concern with matters to do with power and the control of populations and bodies was mirrored in his political activities; he was, throughout his adult life, interested in issues to do with gay rights, prison reform, mental health, and the welfare of refugees. However, there is something slightly paradoxical in this, for it is one of the criticisms of Foucault's work that it functions to undermine any commitment to emancipatory politics. Put simply, the thought here is that by elevating power to the point where it infects everything, Foucault's position rules out the possibility of any genuinely benevolent, or even rational, impulse or intervention. For example, if scientific psychiatry has transformed the lives of "schizophrenics" through the use of antipsychotic drugs, it is only because it is aimed toward the control of patients, not because it seeks good outcomes for them. Or, to take slightly different example, if truth about history is a function of power, then whether or not the Holocaust took place is not a matter of historical fact, but rather a matter of establishing, or not establishing, the dominance of particular historical narratives.

Many of Foucault's critics claim that his views lead straight to a relativism about both truth and morals. For example, Patrick West argued in the *New Statesman*:

> The pervading theme in Foucault's philosophy is that human relations are defined by the struggle for power. Right and wrong, truth and falsehood, are illusions. They are the creation of language and the will to dominate ... Thus, there is no such thing as benevolence: men have created hospitals, schools and prisons not to cure, educate and reform, but to control and dominate 'the Other'. The rationalism of the Enlightenment was merely a mask for this malevolent impulse.

There is certainly something right about this criticism. Indeed, the influence of thinkers like Foucault has been declining in recent years precisely because it has been recognized that their nihilist leanings undermine the possibility of genuine political commitment. Nevertheless, even if one wishes to reject the more radical aspects of Foucault's approach, it would be wrong to dismiss his work in its entirety. Foucault's importance is that he showed how power *can* operate; that is, to create human bodies, human subjects, and populations that in various ways are surveyed, categorized, disciplined, and controlled.

Foucault lived his life as if he were driven by the need to transcend both physical and cultural limits. He lived an extreme lifestyle, and attempted more than once to kill himself, although in the end, he died from an AIDS-related illness.

Writing desk in the home of Michel Foucault.

Glossary

abstraction The practice of dealing with generalized concepts rather than specific, real, or literal events.

abstract reasoning *see* abstraction

aesthetics The branch of philosophy concerned with the nature of beauty, its creation, and its appreciation.

causal Relating to a cause.

communism A political theory originating with Karl Marx, according to which all property should be communally owned, and wealth should be distributed according to individuals' needs.

covenant A contract or agreement drawn up between two or more people.

democracy A system of government in which public policy is decided by the citizens of a state. The views of citizens are usually expressed indirectly, by the election of representatives.

determinism The philosophical view that all events, including human actions, are inevitable because they are dictated by other, preceding events, on the basis of a strict cause-and-effect relationship. Some philosophers have argued that this effectively negates the concept of human free will.

dialectical method A system for resolving a philosophical question by carefully reasoned argument, as famously championed by Socrates. In this system, two speakers adopt opposing viewpoints and take turns to express their arguments; their back-and-forth conversation eventually results in an understanding of the truth.

disputant Someone engaged in an argument or debate.

divine right of kings The theory that monarchs derive their right to rule from the will of God, rather than the will of their subjects.

dualism The philosophical division of reality into two contrasting principles. Descartes famously divided existence into the separate realms of mind and matter.

empiricism The philosophical viewpoint that knowledge can only be established by the experience of the senses.

epistemology The branch of philosophy concerned with knowledge, and how we can distinguish true knowledge from opinion or supposition.

ethics The branch of philosophy concerned with morality, duty, and the conduct of the individual.

existentialism A philosophical movement that elevates to a central position the experiences of the individual, and the expression of their free will.

facticity All the things about an individual that cannot be changed at any given point in time—for example, their age, gender, and genetics.

Hegelian Relating to the philosophical ideas of Georg Wilhelm Friedrich Hegel (1770–1831).

heliocentric Having the sun in the center.

heretical Profoundly opposed to mainstream ideas or beliefs.

heterodoxy A range of opinions other than those espoused by the philosophical mainstream.

humanism A philosophical outlook that elevates human concerns and ideas, rather than spiritual matters or beliefs, to a position of prime importance. Humanists endeavor to understand the world and find solutions to its problems by purely rational means.

interlocutor Someone engaging in a conversation.

Marxist A follower of the political philosophy of Karl Marx (1818–83 CE), who argued that the working class majority was oppressed by the bourgeois minority. He contended that capitalism should be overthrown and replaced by a classless, communist society.

materialism The philosophical doctrine that nothing exists beyond the physical world of matter.

metaphysics The branch of philosophy that addresses the fundamental, underlying nature of existence, the world, time, and space.

nihilism The philosophical position of denying that there is any such thing as objective truth or morality.

panopticon A type of prison with cells arranged in a circle, which allows inmates to be observed at all times, without knowing that they are being observed.

paradigmatically On the basis of a particular system of rules, which underlie a given philosophical position.

proletariat Working class people. In Marxist thought, the proletariat are those people who must sell their labor power.

rationalist Someone who holds to the viewpoint that beliefs about the world must be based on reason rather than emotion or religious faith.

rhetoric The art of effective public speaking, with the goal of persuading others of your argument. The art of rhetoric originated in ancient Greece.

syllogism A form of logical reasoning in which two or more propositions are shown to imply a third proposition. For example, if no fish have fur, and all sharks are fish, then we can conclude that no sharks have fur.

telos The ultimate object, purpose, or goal.

theodicy The philosophical reconciliation of the idea of a good God with the reality of suffering in the world.

theology The systematic study of religion, or the nature of God.

utilitarianism The principle that actions can be justified by the ultimate goal of an exercise.

For Further Reading

Blackburn, Simon. *Being Good: A Short Introduction to Ethics*. New York, NY: Oxford University Press, 2003.
Buckingham, Will et al. *The Philosophy Book*. New York, NY: Dorling Kindersley, 2011.
Dupré, Ben. *50 Philosophy Ideas You Really Need To Know*. New York, NY: Book Sales Inc., 2009.

Web Sites

Due to the changing nature of Internet links, Rosen Publishing has developed an online list of Web sites related to the subject of this book. This site is updated regularly. Please use this link to access the list:

http://www.rosenlinks.com/gph/philo

Index

Acknowledgments

AKG Images: 12, 24, 31, 64, 72, 73, 80, 84, 88, 96, 109, 116

Bridgeman Art Library: 16, 42

Corbis Ltd: 8, 11, 40, 47, 48, 50, 55, 60, 66, 68, 76, 86, 89, 97, 100, 103, 108, 113, 117, 120, 123

Hulton Archive: 19, 28, 32, 52, 104

Lebrecht: 44, 56, 92, 112

Mary Evans Picture Library: 20

Picture Desk/The Art Archive: 23, 34, 36, 37, 57, 61, 83

Shutterstock: 79